Becoming Inclusive

D0898828

Becoming Inclusive

A Worthy Pursuit in Leadership

Helen Abdali Soosan Fagan

*Global Leadership Group
and University of Nebraska-Lincoln*

INFORMATION AGE PUBLISHING, INC.
Charlotte, NC • www.infoagepub.com

Library of Congress Cataloging-in-Publication Data

A CIP record for this book is available from the Library of Congress
http://www.loc.gov

ISBN: 978-1-64802-523-5 (Paperback)
     978-1-64802-524-2 (Hardcover)
     978-1-64802-525-9 (E-Book)

Copyright © 2021 Information Age Publishing Inc.

All rights reserved. No part of this publication may be reproduced, stored in a
retrieval system, or transmitted, in any form or by any means, electronic, mechanical,
photocopying, microfilming, recording or otherwise, without written permission
from the publisher.

Printed in the United States of America

Dedicated to my Parents
Hamzeh Ali Abdali Soosan and Khorshid Yazdanipour Abdali Soosan

You sacrificed everything for us, your children.
I hope this book advances your sacrifices in ways you never imagined.

Contents

Foreword

One of the bedrock principles we have maintained in over 40 years of working in the field of diversity and inclusion is that "diversity is an inside job." Before we can understand and work effectively with others, we have to understand ourselves, our own biases, and our comfort and discomfort with differences. It is only from this solid foundation of self-awareness that we can begin to develop an understanding of others.

Helen's book, *Becoming Inclusive: A Worthy Pursuit in Leadership,* takes this approach. Unlike many books about leading in diverse settings and building environments of inclusion that provide competencies and models, this book takes another path. It helps those aspiring to leadership develop themselves as the tool and use their own vulnerability to connect with others.

Helen uses storytelling, one of the most powerful ways to teach and move others because stories touch our hearts as well as our heads. Her own story is the vehicle she uses to help readers tap into themselves in order to be accessible to others and encourage those they lead to open up to each other. The bonds that are forged when we connect on the personal level are at the foundation of inclusion and the antidote to bias and prejudice. Contact theory supports this when it tells us that prejudice is reduced not by knowledge about other groups, but by the reduction of anxiety that results when we form empathic connections with those who are different. This is the key to building an inclusive environment in the workplace, at home, and in the community.

Becoming Inclusive, pages ix–x
Copyright © 2021 by Information Age Publishing
All rights of reproduction in any form reserved.

This book is both conceptual and practical, providing research and critical information as well as concrete actions readers can take to develop themselves and others. It touches both heart and head as Helen uses vulnerability to explain why this development matters to each of us and then shows us how to do it with examples, questions, and processes to follow. To paraphrase the slogan of the women's liberation movement that the personal is political, the theme for this book could be the personal is organizational. Helen gives us a guide for this continuous improvement process of confronting and sharing ourselves to invite others to do the same so that we can all build lasting environments of inclusion.

—**Lee Gardenswartz, PhD**
Anita Rowe, PhD

Preface

Have you ever tried remodeling a home while still living in it? There is so much chaos. Your life is disrupted with the demolition, the construction, and the cleanup. But you keep moving forward because what you have isn't working anymore.

That is where we are globally.

Now imagine trying to do that without the skill and knowledge to do so, nor a plan to follow for the reconstruction.

The United States of America is a fairly young country when we compare it to the rest of the globe. And since its creation in 1776, about every 100 years, there's been remodeling.

1863, President Lincoln launched a remodel that led to the emancipation of Black men, women, and children as slaves.
1964, President Johnson launched a remodel after pressure from Black men and women to create equal rights.
2020, men, women, and children around the globe are saying no more to the unjust incarceration, and treatment of Black men, women, and children. Further, the U.S. Supreme Court has ruled that the civil rights laws of 1964 apply to the LGBTQ population too.

Each time, people have had to intentionally engage in the work necessary to shift their mindsets to no longer buy and sell Black people as slaves, and to allow Black people equal rights to jobs, housing, buses, education.

Becoming Inclusive, pages xi–xii
Copyright © 2021 by Information Age Publishing
All rights of reproduction in any form reserved.

And now, if we are ever to live up to the ideals upon which this nation was founded, each one of us must intentionally engage in the hard work required to shift our paradigm to create a just and healthy society.

In the pages of the book, I have provided a blueprint—a process by which we assess where we are and intentionally move forward. This is a book I've been writing my entire life. My story as an immigrant and now a non-majority citizen is an example of how I have done that. My research and work in diversity and inclusion, particularly in healthcare, provide models that can be used in organizations and communities ready to pick up their tools, learn new skills, and put in the sweat and emotional equity required to re-imagine and re-build systems that work better for all of us.

Acknowledgments

I am grateful for so many who have helped bring this book to fruition. From students to colleagues, to family, and friends, each person has given me the gift of themselves. What greater gift is there?

Kindra and Cindy, your editorial talents, patience, and wisdom helped me on the days I could write no more, and on the days I wrote words that made no sense.

Fred, you have encouraged me in ways you will never know, and I am eternally grateful to you for connecting me with George and the Information Age Publishing team. Thank you, George, Lisa, and Cindy for answering my questions, and guiding me when I seemed totally lost.

Gina, Marilyn, Rich, Dana, Mary, and Tori thank you for your willingness to read through the pages and provide guidance. You represented the reader, both the leaders and the students who will read through these pages and hopefully find application to their own personal and professional lives.

Thank you to my sister, Helena, for your diligence in helping me find the perfect Persian quotes for each chapter. I loved being able to have you part of the creative aspect of this book.

To our sons, Jonathan and Alan, thank you for putting up with a student for a mom. I always dreamt that my passion for learning would become your passion too and be passed on to your children. Nothing else in my life has taught me more about diversity and inclusion than raising you. You've challenged me and inspired me to become inclusive. I cherish the

Becoming Inclusive, pages xiii–xiv
Copyright © 2021 by Information Age Publishing
All rights of reproduction in any form reserved.

memories we have made and look forward to making new ones with your lovely brides (Liz and Kacy) and your incredible children.

Beckett and Kash, you are the future of our family. I am hopeful that you will grow into young men who have a positive impact on the world around them like your fathers.

Most of all, I thank my favorite human (aka husband) Scott for living every word of this book with me. This book would never have needed to be written had you not stepped up and said, "I will marry you and you don't have to pay me." Your sacrifices and commitment to the promise you made to my dad to make sure I pursue my educational dreams are the reasons we have come this far. I look forward to our future together.

1

Introduction

This book is not a typical leadership textbook with theories and research and data analysis (though it does have some).

It also isn't a typical diversity and inclusion book with philosophies of how we could do things better (though there is some of that, too).

And it isn't a typical autobiography (though I share my personal story as a case study of embracing transformation).

This book is a little of all of the above, and the intended result is a "discussion" that helps the reader (that's you) understand not only the raw realities of how bias and discrimination impact us to the core of our being but the need for inclusion in our world and some ideas how to get there in your own life—and help others get there.

Herein, I offer information and inspiration you can use to address issues of bias, discrimination, and inclusion no matter where you find them. You'll learn a little of the history of bias and discrimination (mostly in health care) in the United States and some of the challenges and obstacles we've faced as a nation. You'll discover concrete actions you can take and

Becoming Inclusive, pages 1–3
Copyright © 2021 by Information Age Publishing
All rights of reproduction in any form reserved.

tools you can use to overcome the challenges of polarized thinking you may encounter every day. Leaders will gain insights from research to develop themselves and then help those they lead. If you are a researcher, there are clues here to potential new paths of research. If you simply want to figure out how to overcome conflicts with family members, friends, coworkers, or others who are different from you or who disagree with you, you will find comfort and ideas here to help.

Above all, my hope in writing this book, is that you see yourself in these pages. That you will realize the power you have to impact change. I hope you are inspired to transform yourself, first and foremost, and then your community (whether that is your town, school, organization, or workplace).

The more I learn, the less I believe I know. With that in mind, this book is not written as an exhaustive study of leadership, diversity, inclusion, or intercultural competence in health care (where I first became interested in diversity) or any other venue or industry. While I bring all of those topics and considerations into the book, I am and shall remain a student of all of these things and more, as we all should be over the remainder of our lives.

Human beings are hurting. We are aching to be seen, heard, understood, appreciated, valued, and given the opportunity to matter. We need only to peruse social media for a glimpse of this ache. As a human, I am no different from any other human in this regard. I've learned that healing comes in part by being able to tell our stories and know they are heard. Our stories matter, because we matter. I have shared a great deal of my own personal story in these chapters in the hope of helping others embrace their own challenges, relieve their pain, and change their lives. I believe our life's purpose is fulfilled when we can turn our pain into something for humanity's gain.

For the last decade of my work as a teacher, I've incorporated personal stories as a key element in developing inclusive leaders. I first learned of this approach to leadership development through two bodies of work: Kevin Cashman's holistic approach to leadership as shared in his seminal book, *Leadership from the Inside Out: Becoming a Leader for Life* (Cashman, 2008) and Robert Quinn's work in internally driven leadership, which you can learn about in his book *Deep Change: Discovering the Leader Within* (Quinn, 1996). I later learned the practical value of personal stories in my study of authentic leadership and transformational leadership theories. As you read the book you now hold in your hands or see on your screen, I urge you to do the work required to understand the power of your own story and become sensitive to the value in other people's stories. It's important to intentionally cultivate an ability to step outside of yourself to understand others. Because, in the words of the French-American poet, Aanis Nin, "We don't see things as they are, we see things as we are."

I would be remiss if I didn't note the impact one specific story has had on me, both personally and in my career: Anne Fadiman's (1997) *The Spirit Catches You and You Fall Down.* This story of a young girl caught in the clash between American health care culture and Hmong culture inspired me when I was working and teaching in the health care world.

In the closing chapter of *The Spirit Catches You,* Arthur Kleinman, offers words that speak to my life's work—helping others examine *their own culture* as a first step on the path to genuine inclusion. He said, "The doctors needed to remember that even their own culture has its own 'set of interests, emotions, and biases.'" Dr. Kleinman is a professor of psychiatry and medical anthropology in global public health at Harvard University. His words ring as true for me today as they did the first time I read them 20 years ago.

In my mind, one of my favorite African proverbs sums up the value of the efforts of all the researchers, practitioners, teachers, leaders, and courageous individuals who have helped us get this far as a species and will help us continue to progress toward a better collective cultural competence: "If you are to go fast, go alone. If you are to go far, go together."

Let us embark on this journey together, for we have far to go.

2

Vulnerability

Destiny forced us to spend our lives this way;
We believe in fate and hold it to be true.

—S.M. Hafiz

We had just arrived in England. Heathrow Airport was bustling with activity, and my brothers and I were restless and excited about the new life ahead of us. My father, whom everyone called Aghayeh Abdali (Mr. Abdali), was the only one of us who spoke English. As he tried to figure out where we needed to go next, we began playing with the rolling luggage cart. Suddenly, the cart got away from us, rolled across the sidewalk and clunked into the side of a taxicab parked at the curb.

The cab driver flung open his door and began yelling—in English, of course. We didn't know what he was saying, and we didn't know what to say back. Agha (Sir), as we affectionately referred to our father, calmly responded to the driver in English, then called us over to sit down on a bench.

"You need to behave," he said gravely. "You must realize you may be the only Iranians people will ever meet. You need to behave in such a way that you represent your family and your country well."

Becoming Inclusive, pages 5–20
Copyright © 2021 by Information Age Publishing
All rights of reproduction in any form reserved.

With those words, I began the painful transition from my life as a native Iranian to my life forever-after as a foreign resident of the United States.

* * *

It was hot outside Detroit's Sinai hospital ICU, but inside it was freezing. I sat at my dad's bedside thinking about my childhood, massaging lotion into his legs and arms, watching his static face for any sign of communication. The stroke he had suffered after heart surgery had taken away his ability to move and speak. There was not much I could do but simply be there with him—and help maintain his body's circulation.

I was desperate to communicate with him, but all he could do in response to my loving words was blink his eyes and produce tears. After much trial and error, we had finally realized he could no longer understand English, the language he had fought so hard for his children to learn. On this day, Agha responded only when we spoke Farsi to him. I fought with my emotions: anger and annoyance, desperation and sorrow, deep love, fear and confusion. My feelings were the only real thing in a surreal environment filled with sterile machines and the stale smell of ailing bodies.

When dad had landed at the Detroit airport a few days earlier, he'd been having chest pains, so my brother had taken him directly to the hospital. The doctors had decided to perform open heart surgery the next day. Our family flew in from around the country to face what would be my father's last among his many struggles.

My brain tried, without much success, to use logic to resolve what was happening. We had been through many terrors and tears as a family, and now we were supposed to be enjoying the conditional peace we had finally won.

How would I live without my Father? How could I let him go so soon? We had only recently been reunited after years of separation. The bitter struggles I had experienced as a result of early isolation from my parents and life in a country where I alternately was seen as a threat and felt threatened, made this moment all the more desperate.

That afternoon, a nurse I hadn't seen before came into the hospital room with a young girl—a student or trainee. The nurse stood near my father's bed, scratching with a pen on his chart. Without introducing herself or explaining her objective, she began asking questions about what he was feeling. She became increasingly frustrated as she waited for my translation into Farsi and then waited for dad to answer as best he could with the blinking of his eyes.

I knew he was frustrated, too, because I could see the tears forming again.

"*Dawg hasti, Aghajan?* Are you hot, dear Agha?" I asked. He blinked.

"He said no," I dutifully relayed to the nurse, my heart sinking with the realization that he must feel trapped within his body.

"*Helenam, meefahmi chi migam?* This is Helen. Do you understand what I'm asking you?" I translated. He blinked.

"Yes, he knows it's me." Did I detect a narrowing of his eyes in love? Tears rolled down his face every time he heard me speak. It broke my heart.

What would typically take seconds, took minutes. The nurse walked away without saying a word. As they passed through the doorway, the nurse leaned over and said to the trainee, "I wish they would learn to speak English. It would make our jobs so much easier."

Anger and horror rose in my chest. My head began to spin as I analyzed the nurse's words. She didn't think my father could speak English. Maybe she thought he was unintelligent and weak. That was so far from the truth. She didn't realize how hard we had worked to learn English and make a life here. She didn't realize what we had been through to get to this place—and how heartbreaking it had been for my father to realize his children would never go back to the country he loved. In my mind, she had insinuated so many things with her words. She had plunged a knife deep into my already broken heart.

The depth of my hurt and heat of my anger compelled me to let go of my father's arm, rise from my seat and follow the nurse through the door and down the hall, fueled by a fever of disdain. I approached her in the hallway from behind, spinning her around with my words. I don't even remember all that I said. Since then, when I talk about it, I describe my diatribe as "verbal vomiting." I'm not proud of the way I behaved. This is not the way I want to represent my family and my country of birth. But, in that moment, I became a slave to my emotions.

"You have no idea who my dad is," I explained, "or what his position was in Iran. How dare you judge him in his condition!" I told her, "He's done and seen more than your puny brain can fathom. He has more intelligence, courage, and dignity in his little finger than you will ever have in your whole brain!"

The nurse apologized for her insensitivity, and I could see she was indeed remorseful, nervous—even afraid of what I might do. But I didn't care. When my dad lost his ability to speak to me and put his arms around me, a big piece of me began to die, and the niceties of social interaction escaped me. I didn't understand my own feelings, let alone have any chance of understanding what had made her say such a thing.

In fact, I was stunned. As a nation, how could we in the United States say we had excellent health care when we had health care providers who were this ignorant? This was not the first time I had experienced this type of ignorance. The nurse's insensitivity dredged up all the sorrow, shame, and pain I had felt so many other times in the years before my father's death, first as an immigrant from what many considered the hostile nation of Iran, then as a minority citizen of the United States.

*   *   *

Flash forward 20 years. I walked rapidly down the hall of Bryan Memorial hospital in Lincoln, Nebraska, a fairly large hospital system with a Level II trauma center, where I led the diversity and cultural competence initiatives. I was heading to a lunch meeting with the hospital chaplain who was also a friend. He would soon meet with several of the hospital's decision makers to get the details of and provide advice related to what ended up being a breakthrough case in culturally adept medical care.

I walked through the door of the cafeteria, took a seat, and settled in to hear the details.

A 12-year-old boy had been hit by a truck while riding a bike in his small-town neighborhood. He had been flown by helicopter to the Bryan trauma center—it was 50 miles away, but it was the closest trauma center to his town. At the hospital, the team sprang into action, doing what they could do to save his life, but his parents were told things didn't look good. The young boy's heart had stopped several times and his brain was showing no activity. He was brain dead.

As a standard part of the process, the family was approached with the question of organ donation. Several hours later, after many tears and much deliberation, the family had informed the chaplain they were ready to re-move life support and would agree to organ donation if the hospital would allow a family member to be present in the operating room at the time of the organ retrieval.

"Help me understand why this is important to you," the chaplain asked the family.

In the faith traditions of their Native American tribe, they believed the spirit of their son rested in his heart. They wanted a family member to be present to observe that the heart would be allowed to fully stop beating and time would be given for the spirit to be freed. This had to happen before the retrieval of organs, so the spirit would not be trapped and go on living in another person's body.

The chaplain had listened to the family, empathized, and reassured them that he appreciated the importance of their request. His next task was to approach hospital decision makers to figure out whether we could legally and logistically grant the family's request.

"I'm not sure how to do this, Helen," he said to me between bites of his sandwich. "I don't know what to say. Can you help me think it through?" His concern was that nothing like this had been done before.

"Remind hospital leaders of the decision we made as an organization," I said slowly, trying to imagine what the objections would be. "Tell them we've made a commitment to respect the culture of our patients. I've been out in the community sharing that commitment in many places—that's why my job was created." I had been hired to be a voice for patients with culture-related needs, as well as assist hospital personnel who didn't have the experience to understand cultural needs other than their own.

The hospital—and many of the organization's individuals in decision-making positions—had gone through a rigorous process of learning about diversity, cultural competence, and inclusiveness. The ethics committee had decided the hospital would meet the cultural needs of any patient as long as it was not against the law.

I reminded the chaplain of some of the examples: We had deactivated overhead sprinklers on a number of occasions so patients could use incense during prayers, and we had, as often as possible, met the request for female staff for Muslim women.

"This is just another example. And it's an opportunity to show our commitment as an organization," I explained. "Tell our decision makers this is a valid cultural need and we must follow through to be true to our commitment to inclusiveness."

After an intense politically and emotionally charged dialogue over the next few hours, we confirmed there were no legal issues connected with meeting this request and the hospital agreed to allow a family member observe recovery of the organs in the operating room. Later, the Nebraska Organ Retrieval System informed the hospital that this was the first time in the 25-year history of organ donation in the state of Nebraska that a Native American family had agreed to organ donation.

I couldn't help thinking back to how things had gone with my dad in the hospital before he died. Why couldn't that situation have gone a little more like this one? I was eager to figure out why this situation with the boy had gone so much better.

In hindsight, the solution to this Native American family's dilemma may seem obvious, but while it was happening it had been extremely unclear what "doing the right thing for the right reasons" would entail. For this organ donation to happen, the doctor and chaplain in the first place had to have had a certain mindset toward the request that the nurse so many years ago had not had. Our hospital administrators had to have embraced the request in spite of its uniqueness and taken it seriously. It stunned me to think how powerful the mindset of everyone involved had been in this critical situation. In cases like this, *the life of a patient and his or her loved ones depends on the unpredictable frame of mind of those in charge.*

As I thought more about it, my mind raced through the implications. The difficulty or ease of dealing with a challenging hospital situation like this lies in the varying experience and mindset of individual medical personnel and hospital administrators, all with different highly specialized duties and widely varied training, background, and motivation. Difficult culture-related medical situations are overcome when those making the decisions and providing the care approach the challenges with a certain level of intercultural sensitivity. But where does that come from?

The answer in this case, at our hospital, had to be that the people involved had been willing to grow in their cultural knowledge and skill with both colleagues and patients long before this young boy became our patient. It wasn't surprising. We had been working as an organization for 4 years toward this kind of cultural competence. I had led Bryan hospital's diversity council through a considerable amount of work to ensure we were delivering culturally competent care. On the ethics committee, my job was specifically to present the lens of diversity and cultural competence in difficult situations like this one.

As the chaplain and I talked quietly over lunch that day, I felt a great sense of satisfaction that our hospital was doing well in this area. I allowed myself a little smile as I left the cafeteria. But I also felt something was missing. I wanted to know more about *what makes people willing* to make these changes. I knew for a fact that some of our staff had not changed as much as I had thought they would. What was the difference for them? And how could the consequences have been different for that dear 12-year-old boy and his family?

There was another consideration for me personally. I asked myself: What had been missing in the knowledge and skill of the nurse who had been so thoughtless that day in my dad's hospital room? I became obsessed with the question. So much so that it became the root of my doctoral coursework and research—and a connecting thread throughout my life.

I didn't know it at the time, but those 2 moments—with the nurse in my father's hospital room and with the Bryan team finding a way to grant the wishes of the young boy's family—would lead me to a career I believe my father would be proud of. I believe I now understand what led the nurse that day to say such a hurtful thing. I've also come to understand what led me to react so violently. I believe I know why the situation with the 12-year-old Native American boy resulted in a breakthrough.

People feel extremely vulnerable when they are out of their comfort zones, especially when they are at their most defenseless—sick or injured—physically and emotionally at the mercy of medical personnel untrained in cultural agility. I've learned how burned out medical personnel become when they are overworked, how helpless they feel when there is nothing more they can do, and how it happens that they voice their frustrations unthinkingly. It's the same in many other areas of life. Diversity—the multidimensional, complex ways humans differ from one another—causes stress, particularly when we are unsure how to navigate the complex layers of differences in relationships. Other overarching considerations can make navigating diversity even more difficult: organizational structures, cultural dynamics, personal power.

I've had the honor of exploring diversity alongside hundreds of students, social scientists, psychologists, community leaders, and business leaders. I have uncovered new ways for human beings to successfully work and live with those who are different from themselves. As the world becomes a more cohesive global community, we are going to need these skills more often. Our ability to successfully navigate diversity will become more and more important. We will find ourselves in increasingly more complex and more numerous diverse situations, and it will demand a different approach than the one both the nurse and I took that day in the hospital.

In their book, *Leadership in a Diverse and Multicultural Environment*, authors Mary Connerly and Paul Patterson (2005) reinforce the idea that boundaries between diverse people are being shattered: "National boundaries no longer define the world of organizations. The free movement of labor continues to intensify as organizations diversify geographically" (p. 2). Large and small companies around the world interact with customers and employees from multiple nations. This includes companies ranging from GM, Budweiser, Disneyworld, and Medtronic, to Apple, IBM, Google, and HSBC in many different industries.

According to the research firm McKinsey Global Institute (Manyika et al., 2014), the global flow of goods, services, and finance reached $26 trillion in 2012 or 36% of global GDP—1.5 times the GDP of 1990. "They say that 1 in 3 goods now crosses national borders and more than 1/3 of financial investments are international transactions. In the next decade, global flows could triple, powered by rising prosperity and participation in the emerging world and by the spread of the Internet and digital technologies" (para. 2). McKinsey projected that global flows would reach between $54 trillion and $85 trillion by 2025, more than double or triple flows of 2012.

Meeting the demands of this global integration is easy in some ways—many citizens of the world have wanted this coming together of people for a long time. However, there is a hurdle that can keep us from successfully seeing ourselves as a global community: An inability to overcome our personal biases so we can interact in positive ways with those who are different from ourselves. We need to develop the psychological capacity and emotional intelligence to deal with our own personal issues that often lead us to misunderstandings with others. We need help to understand our own thoughts and emotions before we can see the world through eyes other than our own. We need to learn how to *ask questions* rather than making assumptions.

When we "don't know what we don't know" about people who are different from us, we often instinctually fall back to a position of suspicion. We draw on the only thing we do know: our own experiences and the common beliefs of our own culture. We fear a repeat of past hurts, and every unknown situation holds a *memory of pain* that comes from these past hurts. It takes a great measure of courage to be authentic with our own pain and vulnerabilities, to unravel the way they hold us hostage and keep us from becoming leaders who can effectively bridge differences.

Can it be done? Daily news is still rife with attacks and killings motivated by misunderstandings related to race, gender, and class. Government officials must navigate delicate negotiations between feuding countries. Pastors find they must moderate disagreements between ethnic groups who want to worship in different ways. Teachers find themselves refereeing conflicts between students of diverse backgrounds. Families face clashes related to gender, income—even politics and religious beliefs. Elderly people are misunderstood, neglected, and abused.

Each and every one of us must find a way to deal with differences at whatever level they appear in our daily lives. We all must face our own hesitation and inability to overcome and heal our personal memories of pain and find a better way. Then, after we learn how to do this, it is our responsibility—and privilege—to teach others.

The first step is understanding what makes us who we are.

*   *   *

I was born in Masjed Soleyman, Iran, on July 31, 1964, the second of four children. Until the age of 16, I had only two brothers. My baby sister was born in Iran much later, when I was living away from my family in the United States.

On Kharg Island, when I was a child, we lived in a modern ranch-style home. It was like any American ranch-style home of the 1960s, but it was filled with beautiful Persian rugs and artifacts from around the world that my dad had brought back from his travels. We had everything we needed in our cozy home, including a gardener and a maid to help my mother. She was sophisticated, fashion-minded, and well-dressed—like Jackie O and Sophia Loren. Our large yard was filled with flowers and banyan trees. My brothers and I liked swinging from vines on the trees, and I enjoyed watching my dad tend to his beloved flowers.

My father admired Western culture, education, and health care, though he also felt pride in our own history, customs, and culture. Among the breathtaking natural, cultural, and architectural landmarks in our temperate Middle Eastern country, my family and many others lived a life of prosperity. We never had to do without. We were accepted, loved, and comfortable in our world.

My parents and siblings and I enjoyed strong ties with a large extended family. We often visited my grandparents' humble home in Masjed Soleyman, where they raised chickens and goats and maintained a small number of fruit trees.

Summer was my favorite time of year. When we gathered with my aunts, uncles, and cousins, we ate, danced, and listened to lots of stories. I knew my cousins well enough that it seemed as if they were my brothers and sisters. Most evenings, while the adults talked of world issues, we played until the sun went down. We slept peacefully under the stars on the rooftop, knowing all of these people would love and support us no matter what life brought our way.

My father was admired and respected by our family and by everyone he worked with. At the National Iranian Oil Company, he advanced through the ranks of the company and earned his position on Kharg Island, which was a major oil exporting location in the northwestern corner of the Persian Gulf. Dad was head of the personnel department, in charge of the hiring and development of oil exploration and exportation teams. He hired people from all over the world. Through his exposure to different people, places, and cultures, he saw the value of knowing multiple languages and making a special effort to learn about the world. He was an inclusive leader without knowing what that was. We moved to several different cities to accommodate my father's position with the oil company, but most of my memories are of Kharg Island.

Because English was and still is the standard international language for business and science, my dad taught himself enough English to speak fluently with those he hired from other nations. I would listen to him speak English with his colleagues and friends from across the globe, and I became determined to someday speak the language, too. My family laughed at me as I pretended to speak English like my dad.

When my dad came home from the oil company at night, he was no longer an important international employment liaison. He was just my dad. He sat with me for make-believe tea parties and calmed my fears by telling me stories about a loving and hardworking family of mice. He picked me up, danced around the room with me in his arms, and sang nonsensical songs, calling me his *holoo koochooloo*—his little peach. We often watched American television together. I was in love with the *Six Million Dollar Man* and swore I would someday speak English like Lee Majors.

As dad learned more about the world, he developed a strong desire to provide the same knowledge and advantages for his children—a similar exposure to the world. My parents wanted us to receive an excellent education. They dreamed of sending us to college in England and were convinced we would be more successful if we learned English at an early age. For that reason, my father explained, we would soon move to England to attend primary school. Though this is what many cosmopolitan, affluent Iranian families were doing, my parents' extended families were against our move, especially because my brothers and I were so young. But no one could talk my parents out of it.

> *Journal Entry:*
> *Saturday, January 7, 1977*
>
> On this day My DaDDy had
> gone and I do not Know when
> can I See him again When he
> gone I Was Very Sad and blew.
> Helen Soosan

In 1976, when I was 12 and my brothers were 11 and 13, my parents put their plan into motion: For the next few years, my mother and brothers and I would live and study in England during the school year, then return to Iran in the summers. Even my mother would attend school to finish what she hadn't been able to complete before getting married. My father would continue working in Iran to pay for our schooling. As we each completed college, we would move back to Iran and continue our lives there to live and work among our nation's leaders.

Oblivious to the fact that my parents' dream would die with the up-heaval of our home country during 1978 and 1979, we left for England. It was exciting at first, but reality set in when I realized my dad—my knight in shining armor, storyteller, and friend—would not be with us for long.

Suddenly, I was in a new land, learning a new language, adjusting to a new culture—without the person who gave me strength and made me confident in myself: my dad. During the first summer, we each stayed with a different family during the week to immerse ourselves in the language. It wasn't easy. English is a funny language to learn. I remember hearing about "butterflies in someone's stomach" and I wondered how they got there.

When school began, for the first time in my life I was not accepted with-out question. The English children made fun of the way I talked, the way I dressed, the color of my skin. They even made fun of the way I smelled because of the food I ate at home. It was a rude awakening for my daddy's little princess, who had grown up to that point with everything she needed and had always been treated with love and respect.

I wasn't sure how to respond to the insults, so I looked at it philosophi-cally. I let it make me stronger. I vowed to someday speak English so well that no one would be able to tell it was my second language. If you know me today, you know I have accomplished this goal.

In 1977, my mom's youngest brother, Mehrzad, moved to England to attend college. He saved the day for us! He made being in England fun. He could drive, so he took my brothers and me everywhere. Mehrzad, who was a kind and generous young man, temporarily filled the emptiness left by the absence of my dad. He took our minds off of the things other children said about us, and we pushed our feelings deep inside.

It was never my father's intention that we would move away from Iran and not return. We didn't need another country to help us prosper. My parents were already wealthy. We had a great life; they simply wanted to find a place for us to get the world's best education and to expand our worldview. We immigrated legally and thought it would be temporary. I remember thinking it was strange that we were residents on one side of a border and immigrants on the other.

Migration has been part of the history of human beings in all areas of the world. People have always moved away to gain better access to food, water, and grazing for their animals. Limiting people's movement from one nation to another is a relatively recent construct in the thousands of years humans have been on this planet.

In some cases, people don't move, but boundaries do, instantly turning residents into immigrants or vice versa. The United States, for example, engulfed a part of Mexico that today comprises the states of Texas and California.

Some people are forced into migration to escape war and violence. Others choose to migrate to new areas to get better access to jobs, health care, and education. Just as my family did when we left Iran.

The Summer of 1978, when I was 14 years old, was the last time I was in Iran until many years later, after I was married and no longer an Iranian citizen. We went home in 1978 to see family and friends. I enjoyed showing off my genuine English ability (no more pretending) and seeing my cousins again. They were impressed with what I had learned.

There was something different about my home country that summer, though. When we landed in Tehran, I saw tanks and armed men in the streets. My dad and the male members of my extended family were constantly talking about the Shah, the Ayatollah, the SAWAK (Iranian Secret Service), and the United States. My family members, while not political, were educated and engaged in intelligent debates about global issues. For me, this time was a mixture of joy and intense concern.

When we returned to England at the end of that summer, the British government informed us they would not renew our visas when they expired at the end of 1979. We would have to return to the unrest of Iran and abandon my parents' plan to educate us in the West—or we would have to find another country that allowed foreign students. My parents already had sacrificed so much, and they didn't want to give up on their dream. My dad had friends all over the world and believed he could find another place for us to receive an excellent education, so he began to search.

Several of dad's friends and his Iranian cardiologist had moved to America. They provided information about places we could go to school in the United States. Two of my mom's brothers already were studying at American colleges. Regardless of their own positive experiences there, my uncles begged my father not to bring any of us to America—especially me. They didn't believe the American lifestyle would be good for young children.

My parents, again going against the wishes of others, decided we would simply transfer our original English-speaking education plan to the United States.

It was a good idea, but it was not to be—at least not in the form we had hoped. The U.S. Embassy in London would not issue a visa to my mother that would allow her to stay with us in the United States. My parents were issued only visitor's visas with time enough allotted to get us settled in the boarding school, then they would have to return to Iran.

And thus began a new chapter of my life that would test me to the core.

* * *

The United States of America has had a conflicted relationship with newcomers for more than four centuries. From the time of our nation's early settlers and the launching of the slave trade in the 1600s (which lasted until 1808), to Irish and German settlement (1820–1870) and immigration of the Chinese during the Gold Rush, then the influx of Eastern Europeans (1880–1920) and the desperate immigration of the Jewish population during WWII, most of us can trace our roots back to a ship or plane that brought our ancestors here.

Countless Mexican Americans are citizens of this country, not because their ancestors immigrated but because the national boundary lines moved. In the southern United States, this began when Texas gained its independence from Mexico in 1836 and became part of the Union in 1845, and it ended with the close of the Mexican–American War. In 1848, with the Treaty of Guadalupe, the state of Hidalgo in Mexico ceded to the United States about 525,000 square miles of territory that now lies in California and the Southwest (Utah, Arizona, New Mexico, Nevada, and parts of Colorado and Wyoming).

Between 1860 and 1920, the immigrant share of the total U.S. population fluctuated between 13% and a peak of 14.8% in 1890, mainly due to high levels of European immigration. Restrictive immigration legislation in 1921 and 1924, coupled with the Great Depression and World War II, led to a sharp drop in new arrivals. As a result, the foreign-born portion of Americans steadily declined between the 1930s and 1970s, reaching a record low of about 5% in 1970. After 1970, the number of U.S. immigrants more than quadrupled, growing to 13.3% of the U.S. population in 2014 (Batalova et al., n.d.).

According to the Institute of International Education (IIE), in the 2014–2015 academic year, more than 974,900 international students were attending American colleges and universities, contributing $30.5 billion to the U.S. economy, representing more than 373,000 jobs (Witherell, 2015).

It's fairly obvious that most people who enter the United States from other places have a vision of America as being an incredible place of opportunity and growth. My father was no different. He expected we would experience wonderful adventures and meet inspiring people in our lives here. He revered everything about the United States: its education, health care, engineering, architecture, and technological advancements. He believed those who found their way to the United States would have the opportunity to be free—to be themselves. He loved the idea that women living in the United States had just as much opportunity to become educated as men. He loved the ideals upon which the United States was founded.

Unfortunately, the truth often is far from the vision.

Actor Will Smith, in the movie *The Concussion*, playing the role of Bennet Ifeakandu Omalu, a real-life Nigerian physician who emigrated to the United States, explains how this unsettling phenomenon affected him: "When I was in Nigeria, the U.S. was close to heaven and Nigeria was below it. Now that I'm living here, I am in so much pain."

*   *   *

At the tender age of 15, after landing in New York City on a Pan Am airliner with my mother, father, and brothers, we began driving south. It would be hours before we would reach Florida Central Academy in the town of Sorrento. At first, I was excited. The summer before, I had seen the movie *Grease*, and I thought that's what our new life in the United States would be like. I expected to have fun and meet exciting new friends—and of course learn everything my father wanted me to learn, as well as perfect my English speaking and writing.

As we traveled toward Florida, it began to sink in that my mother would not be with us and I would only see my brothers sporadically, because they would live in the boys' dorm and I would live in the girls' dorm. I became sadder with every mile of city and country that passed by as I watched through the windows of the car. I was afraid of being alone—and even more afraid when I thought about living and studying with other boarding school students from all over the world.

In my first days within the confines of the academy, I could only think of myself. I was consumed by fear and anger. Before my parents left, I remember having a major meltdown in the dormitory. Why would they leave me? Would they ever really come back for me? What was there for me in this strange place? "Nothing!" I thought. It didn't help that I was a teenager, naturally full of questions about myself and worries about everything, from the strange changes my body had been going through to my unseen future.

Today, after many years of thinking, analyzing, and discussing with my parents, I now understand that those days in Florida were some of the most difficult of their own lives as well, as they contemplated their forced return to Iran. I admire the courage it took to leave their 14-, 15- and 16-year-old children thousands of miles. Even then, their intent was that we would return to Iran someday and make our country a better place.

In a matter of days, culture shock settled over me. Many things I thought of as normal became "weird," because they were so different from England and Iran. My roommates shaved their underarms and legs. They wore makeup, had boyfriends, smoked cigarettes, and drank. I didn't do any of those things and, because I refused to, they made fun of me. It felt much like the ridicule I had endured in England. For the first time, I felt a *memory of pain associated with being different*. Because of the painful experiences I had endured in England, I made unfavorable assumptions about Florida, the United States, and the people living around me.

I begged my dorm mom, Mrs. Louise Anderson, to let me move in with 2 older Iranian girls, Farah and Sophia, and she allowed this. We were all new arrivals in the United States. I taught them to speak English, and they protected me. They became the family I was missing—and so did my dorm mom. Before my parents left for Iran, they had asked Mrs. Anderson to promise she would watch over me, give me a piece of fresh fruit every day, and teach me how to do my own laundry.

I found two places I felt comfortable at the academy: the library and the stables. I'd had horseback riding lessons in England and I knew how to take care of the magnificent animals. I spent many hours brushing down my favorite, Socks. I would sit on the fence and talk to him, telling him how sad I was or describing the events of the day. I felt a connection with him, because he was gentle—and I needed any possible connection I could find with a gentle thing. The horses and books helped me slow down and calm myself. They were the only things that felt familiar. Nothing else looked, felt, smelled, or tasted like anything I had known before.

Questions

1. Crucible moments are moments that leave a lasting impact on the person and somehow shift the person's identity. Can you think of a crucible moment in your life that tested the core of who you are? How did it impact you? Who are you as a result of that moment?
2. Whom would you not want your children to bring home and introduce as their future spouse? Why?
3. Whom would you be afraid to bring home and introduce as your future spouse? Why?
4. How do the answers to Questions 2 and 3 impact your decisions? Your friend choices? The neighborhood you live in? The people you vote for? The people you call friend?
5. Have you ever had a moment where you realized suddenly that your "normal" was actually "different"? What was that experience like?

3

The Health Care Dilemma

That heart which stands aloof from pain and woe
No seal or signature of Love can show.

—A. J. Arbery

An elderly Afghani woman was brought to the emergency room of Bryan Health with abdominal pain she had been experiencing for quite some time. The woman, who was accompanied by her daughter and son-in-law, did not comprehend any English. She had come to Lincoln, Nebraska, from Afghanistan as a refugee to settle with her daughter's family. She had been forced to leave her homeland as a result of the war on terror that commenced after New York's World Trade Center was attacked September 11, 2001. The woman's daughter and son-in-law spoke very little English. They were taking classes to learn English, but it was proving very difficult for the woman's daughter to learn the complicated new language. Neither woman could read or write—even in their native tongue.

The woman was admitted to the hospital, and a few days later was diagnosed with end-stage cancer.

Becoming Inclusive, pages 21–33
Copyright © 2021 by Information Age Publishing
All rights of reproduction in any form reserved.

Over the next few days, it became apparent to health care workers at the hospital that circumstances would make this a more challenging case than usual. Because the woman was Muslim, modesty during physical examinations was required and the family requested a female physician. Further complicating the case was the fact that the daughter and son-in-law were unwilling to discuss end-of-life issues with the patient. They would not openly talk with her about her impending death.

To properly care for this elderly woman, hospital staff had to go outside of their personal comfort zones and uncover creative solutions to provide culturally and linguistically appropriate care. It was imperative that the woman's medical care would include culturally competent interpreter staff, with translated written materials the son-in-law could read and explain to his wife. Clinical and support staff who knew how to ask about and negotiate cultural issues had to conduct culturally sensitive discussions with the family about treatment consent and advance directive forms—even appropriate food choices.

When the elderly woman died, the family requested time to wash and anoint her body with special oils. No one had asked to do this before. The hospital staff wasn't sure how to respond or manage the request—they weren't used to allowing family members to handle the body of the deceased. When a patient dies in an American hospital, the rules say the body can't be released to anyone but funeral home officials. The staff had worked hard to accommodate all of the family's needs when the patient was alive, but there was no context for accommodating this last request within the rules and practices of this American hospital so far away from the country of the woman's birth. I received a phone call late one weekend night asking me to help with the family's request.

According to Muslim tradition, I told the department manager, it's necessary for the family of the deceased to anoint the body with camphor oil, then wrap it in cloth at the burial site and put it into a wooden box. The manager and her staff had never heard of this tradition. Even the hospital chaplains were at a loss. I compared the family's request with death traditions of the Christian faith in the United States—a tradition more familiar to most staff members at the hospital.

I explained that when a person dies in the United States, the body typically is embalmed (using embalming fluid) and prepared by the funeral home, so the person looks as close as possible to how he or she looked in life. In much the same way, anointing a body with oil and wrapping it in cloth is typical for people of the Muslim faith in most countries. The point of reference comparing camphor oil with the embalming fluid of their own culture helped the staff understand the reasons for the oil, as well as the importance of this tradition to the family. This understanding eliminated their fear of the unknown. In this situation, I served as a cultural interpreter, providing our staff a way to understand the behavior and decision-making process of their patient's family.

Once the staff had a better context for understanding, they wanted to help. They were able to ask questions that would allow them to accommodate the family's needs. Instead of feeling inconvenienced and asking, "Why do they want to do this?"; the staff began to ask questions such as: "How can we get the oils they need? Is it possible to put them in touch with other people in the community who know and can support their traditions?" The hospital staff, although they certainly were aware there was a cultural difference at play, simply had been feeling frustrated that they couldn't help their patient. The family, although they most certainly realized their loved one was being cared for by people unfamiliar with their traditions, simply had been feeling frustrated and fearful that they might not be able to carry out the requirements of their religion and say goodbye to their mother properly.

* * *

Conflicts in a health care setting are some of the most difficult to manage, especially when cultures collide. I discovered this in my own experience with the nurse during my dad's last days. When injured or ill people enter a hospital or clinic, they are hurting, uncomfortable, and sometimes afraid. For caregivers, it may be all in a day's work, but for patients' emotions are heightened and it's a difficult time with unusual issues to overcome. Some of the patient's cognitive abilities decline due to stress, anxiety, and fear of the unknown, which further escalates the tension and frustration of both patient and caregiver.

To make matters more complicated, when patients enter the hospital or clinic, they usually have specific expectations of the way they will be treated. Many times, those expectations aren't verbalized, because patients assume hospital staff share their vision of the way treatment should go. Patients often think, "Because I'm a human being and you are a human being, you should know what I need." The problem is that we each operate with our own set of assumptions—health care providers, patients, and family members. Health care providers, who are educated, knowledgeable, and committed to their profession, sometimes believe their medical knowledge supersedes patient expectations. Even culturally aware and culturally agile hospital staff sometimes forget the patient is the best expert on the needs of his or her own body.

Communication is the key to overcoming these conflicts and misunderstandings. In the book *Intercultural Communication* by Larry Samovar and Richard Porter (1997), the authors define intercultural communication as any time "the parties to a communication act bring with them different experiential backgrounds that reflect a long-standing deposit of individual or group experience, knowledge and values" (p. 4). The word "long-standing" is a clue to why intercultural communication is so difficult. Every person's background is deeply embedded with certain habits of communication.

Samovar and Porter (1997) explain that communication in the health care environment is complicated because layers of culture intersect, and cultural layers are different for each and every person involved, including medical providers, patients, family members, pastors, and social workers. The layers of culture include:

- overall culture of health care;
- unique culture of each area of health care (e.g., nurse culture, physician culture, non-clinical culture);
- ethnic/national traditions and the deep-rooted values associated with a patient's country of origin, race, or religion; and
- expectations shaped from each individual's personal experiences, both positive and negative.

If we add the volatility and trauma of life-and-death situations, we have a complex combination of conditions ripe for painful misunderstanding. Emotion is the fuel that feeds this fire. Dr. R. W. Brislin (2000), in his book, *Culture's Influence on Behavior*, said human beings have their strongest emotional reactions when their culture's values are either violated or ignored.

Most of us in Western cultures are socialized to avoid pain, so it's not surprising that no one wants to talk about the issues causing emotional, culture-related pain in medical settings. In my opinion, this is what has led to disparities in health care.

Statistically, disparity in health care continues. According to the 2015 National Health Care Quality and Disparities Report, access to quality care still is an issue for Black and Hispanic populations. Income plays a role in this, but a White population of lower socioeconomic status doesn't fare as badly as Blacks and Hispanics of lower socioeconomic levels (Agency for Healthcare Research and Quality, 2016). We see evidence of similar disparities in housing (Herbert et al., 2005), and the legal system. Such disparities are noted in numerous sources, such as *The New Jim Crow* by Michelle Alexander (2012) and *Just Mercy* by Bryan Stevenson (2014) in which multiple cases are cited. We also see this in the faith sector of society, where, in the words of Reverend Martin Luther King Jr., "It is appalling that the most segregated hour of Christian America is 11:00 on Sunday morning" (Meet the Press, 1960).

Solutions for disparity in every segment of society lie on two tracks—that of the individual and that of the system. Systemic change cannot happen without individual growth. To change the system, individuals must develop new insights about themselves, develop the ability to shift their perspectives of other people, and gain a willingness to engage in the hard work of systemic change in health care, housing, law, and communities. Individual growth will not impact systemic change unless we are all willing to do this together. Most caregiving individuals I've come across in health care genuinely are willing to do the work and want to help patients who are filled with fear, anxiety, and a real desire to be understood. For all of these reasons, health care provides a laboratory for understanding diversity and finding solutions.

Culture-based questions in medicine, such as those raised by the needs of the Afghani woman and her family, are becoming more commonplace, because the world is becoming more interconnected. Patients are more likely today to find themselves being cared for by medical staff who are influenced by a different culture than their own. This has underscored disparities in health care to an increasing degree. As awareness has risen, the complicated challenges of accommodating culture within the health care environment have been examined more often in modern studies and books.

In *The Spirit Catches You and You Fall Down*, the story of young Lia Loc, a Hmong Chinese toddler suffering from epilepsy, researcher Anne Fadiman (1998) examines the clash between cultures that affected Lia's treatment. The conflict Fadiman studied over the course of more than a decade involved the beliefs and traditions of social workers and hospital staff at a small mid-American hospital and the many ways those beliefs contrasted with the vastly different beliefs and culture of Lia's Hmong family.

Fadiman's (1998) book is filled with accounts of events and struggles that demonstrate the misunderstanding, miscommunication, and distrust between Lia's professional caregivers and her family. The decisions made both by Lia's parents and her doctors may or may not have led to numerous crises of care on the one hand and the unexpected lengthening of the child's life on the other. Her professional caregivers believed the power of Western medicine would help her most, but Lia's family preferred the power of animal sacrifices. It had worked for them in China—why wouldn't it work in the United States? They believed the illness itself was simply *qaug dab peg* (the spirit catches you and you fall down), the wandering of her soul.

Patients aren't the only ones who experience medical disparity. Providers face their own crises of culture. Many of their challenges are beyond the scope of this book, but other authors have addressed them. In the book, *Black Man in a White Coat: A Doctor's Reflections on Race and Medicine*, author Damon Tweedy, MD (2016), examines the challenges Black doctors face, as well as the health burdens plaguing Black patients. His story becomes deeply personal, because he has not only studied and come up through the ranks as a Black doctor, hearing constantly about the odds against good health for Blacks, but he is then diagnosed with a chronic disease found in much higher proportions within the Black community. The goal in telling his story is to humanize those unfavorable medical statistics. He doesn't claim to have answers but believes shedding light on his own experiences can add to the dialogue and ultimately—he hopes—contribute to improved health for all Black people.

Both of these books and the stories of the people in them imply that solutions for overcoming health disparity are rooted in something personal, not just the science of medicine or the practices of medical institutions. A patient's situation, emotion, and ability to cope are dependent on that unique individual's many layers of expectation—which are indelibly linked to the many layers of culture that influence and define them, as well as layers of culture that have influenced them in the past. The way patients behave in a medical setting can be influenced by their family history, work environment and coworkers, religious beliefs, peers, geographical setting, good or bad past experiences with medical staff and medical settings—even age and gender. The same can be said of the medical personnel who treat those patients.

It can be very difficult for members of the majority race, nationality, or culture to fully understand the damage being done in a disparate medical setting and feel motivated to participate in solutions that truly make things better. If you are an American born-and-raised, perhaps of the majority race, seeking medical care in your own country and being treated by members of your own race, age, or gender, you are unlikely to understand on a personal level—or even recognize—medical disparity. You may have no way to instantly understand that a member of a minority group seeking care within the U.S. medical network is experiencing overwhelming disconnectedness and fear of things unknown.

*   *   *

Imagine a future in which the United States and Canada are at odds. Canada becomes the aggressor in the conflict and Canadians begin to hate the United States and its citizens. Over a couple of decades, the problem escalates and physical conflicts between Canadians and U.S. citizens near the border become violent. Your family lives in the southern part of Montana where there are wide open spaces and little worry about the violence. Most members of your family watch news of the conflict with interest, but they think of it as someone else's problem and they don't really pay close attention.

Suddenly, the conflict spills over the border. Canada has enlisted help from other U.S. haters around the world. Canadians already have secretly begun to overtake small rural U.S. communities, and then suddenly, with one coordinated military initiative, Canada and its allies take control of the U.S. capitol, secure strategic metropolitan locations around the country, and effectively conquer the country. One of the conquerors' first priorities is eliminating people of German descent. Canada, now a communist nation, has begun ethnic cleansing to prepare the conquered nation for its own citizens and allies around the globe.

It doesn't seem real, but it is all happening around you in spite of your disbelief. German Americans are disappearing in large numbers, and if they resist, they are killed on the spot. Everyone in your German American family is murdered except you, your husband, and your mother. The trauma is making it difficult to make decisions, but your husband convinces you the only hope the three of you have of remaining alive is to escape to Mexico. You pack your bags, taking only the bare necessities, and you all make the long journey from Montana to the Mexican border. You request and are granted asylum. You are some of the first to arrive—and you get there just in time, Mexico anticipates a potential massive influx of U.S. citizens over the next year and with regret decides to close its borders to avoid overburdening the country's infrastructure.

You, your husband, and your mother are sent to a Mexican city willing to accept you as refugees, where you are given jobs and assistance on one condition: that you quickly learn the language and become working residents so you can take care of yourselves. You begin taking Spanish classes, but before you are able to communicate competently, your mother gets extremely sick. She's in terrible pain, and you rush her to the hospital.

How would you want her to be treated? What provisions of care would you want for her? Do you believe the hospital in Mexico would offer the same services and forms of care you were used to in the United States? How would it feel if a nurse ridiculed you and your mother for not speaking Spanish? Now imagine your mom is diagnosed with cancer and dies while she's in the hospital far away from home. How will you feel if the medical staff can't understand how to help you carry out the important traditions of your family and your faith? If you are used to American end-of-life customs, what will you do if you can't find a funeral home to embalm or cremate her body?

*   *   *

As a country, the United States is still on an uphill climb when it comes to successfully managing and overcoming health care disparity. However, there is no doubt it's better than it used to be. Government mandates require interpreter services, and communication and culture must be part of providing patient-centered care. The level of culturally competent care depends on the specific hospital and people involved. Overall, there seems to be greater knowledge of religious and cultural differences—and information about non-majority cultures is more easily obtained than it used to be. The presence of knowledge doesn't mean behavior will change, but it's a start.

Let's step back into history for a moment to examine the roots of health care disparity. The stories you are about to hear seem horrifying to us in the 21st century, but they explain a great deal about the unconscious tendencies of human beings to protect ourselves, as well as our blind spots, and our inclination to act on our fears. It sometimes took decades of study, analysis, protest, and politics to right some of these wrongs. The fallout from events like these has left us with lingering disparities that we often find difficult to explain. On a fundamental level, these accounts of real events demonstrate why it's so difficult sometimes to overcome differences between us.

The first account is of Henrietta Lacks, a young Black mother of five children in Maryland. In 1950, Henrietta was diagnosed with an aggressive form of cervical cancer. During her operation, two cervical tissue samples were taken by the doctors from her body without her knowledge and used in research.

Henrietta's story was told by author Rebecca Skloot (2010) in her 2010 book, *The Immortal Life of Henrietta Lacks*. In her book, Skloot explains that Henrietta's tissue was given to Doctor George Otto Gey, a researcher at Johns Hopkins Hospital in Baltimore. He discovered that Henrietta's cells reproduced at a much higher rate than normal cells and could be intentionally divided many times without dying, a very unusual condition that made the cells ideal for conducting experiments. Most cells survive only for a few days, which makes it difficult to test them.

After Henrietta's death, Dr. Gey launched a commercial line of cells from the samples without notifying the Lacks family of this activity. At the time, it wasn't illegal to sell or use discarded tissues taken from a person's body during a medical procedure. In the following years and decades, Henrietta's resilient cells continued to be divided and used for experiments by medical researchers, labs, and doctors around the world. Because the cell line could be indefinitely perpetuated, the cells became known as "immortal" cells and were given the name HeLa, a scientific name derived using a common method of labeling cells with the first two letters of the donor's first and last names.

Eventually, Henrietta's immortal cells led to a number of important biomedical breakthroughs and creation of a multimillion-dollar industry. HeLa cells were used in development of the polio vaccine by Jonas Salk, who mass-produced the cells for the first time in a cell production factory. According to my research (Wikipedia, n.d.), the cells have been used to research cancer, AIDS, gene mapping, radiation, and toxic substance effects, as well as testing human sensitivity to certain manufactured products. It has been estimated that scientists have grown 20 tons of HeLa cells and filed nearly 11,000 related patents.

When a large number of the cells became contaminated, Henrietta's family became aware that the doctor had harvested and sold her tissue. Members of the medical community contacted the family and asked for blood samples they hoped would replace the contaminated cells.

Henrietta's story has become a landmark case in both medical ethics and cultural bias as related to treatment for non-majority patients. In her book, Skloot uses the case of Henrietta's cells to help readers understand the human side of science experimentation and why many patients distrust the American health care system. Unethical experimentation on human patients has become unacceptable in the 21st century. However, the distrust remains for many entering the health care system.

How would you have felt if Henrietta had been your mother? What if the woman on the operating table had been the doctor's mother? Would the decision have been made to take the tissue samples in the first place if? If Henrietta had been a member of the majority race, do you believe her family would have been informed and compensated once it was discovered the cells had such far-reaching potential? Who was making all of these decisions—or failing to make decisions?

In the United States and many other places in the world, if a corporation makes a mistake, the assets of the corporation are legally attached to provide a remedy. Unless criminal actions were taken by an individual, the people who made decisions related to the mistake are not held liable. The fact remains, however, that the mistake was made by people. And it is people who must learn from the mistake and make different decisions.

When it comes to health care, not to mention cultural disparities in many other areas of life, if change is going to happen, it's true that institutional policies and the way they are implemented and enforced must change. But it's people who must first be willing to change themselves and then be willing to initiate institutional changes.

* * *

The question of human experimentation without a patient's knowledge is the most prominent aspect of Henrietta Lacks' story. But there is another aspect to her story that has raised questions about the decisions that were made. It's impossible to hear the story today without wondering whether Henrietta's race or socioeconomic status influenced the doctor's decision not to inform her family about the phenomenal properties of her cells—especially after the cells became widely used for prominent medical breakthroughs. The decision could have been made to share this information with her family at many points along the way, by many different people. Why did no one decide to reach out to the family? There is not any way to know this, but we have many other examples of race-related health care disparities to indicate the answer often has to do with differences in power and privilege—and sometimes money.

Another famous example of health care disparity has its origins at the Tuskegee Institute in Tuskegee, Alabama (U.S. Public Health Service Syphilis at Tuskegee, 2015). In 1895, Booker T. Washington, then president of Tuskegee Institute, in an Atlanta speech, laid out his dream for "Black economic development." His vision was embraced by White leaders, especially Julius Rosenwald, president of Sears, Roebuck and Company, who agreed to provide financial support for the institute.

The goal of the institute and the hope of its funders was to enhance the education and training of the America's Black population—in itself, an admirable endeavor. In 1926, after Mr. Washington's death, the work continued under the leadership of Robert Motin. During that time, the institute identified health as a factor limiting Black economic development. In particular, syphilis was a major concern. Thirty-five percent of Blacks in their reproductive years suffered from the disease.

In 1932, the Tuskegee Institute began a study in partnership with the U.S. Public Health Service to understand and trace the natural history of syphilis in order to get funding for treatment programs for the Black population. Participants in the "Tuskegee Study of Untreated Syphilis in the Negro Male" originally included 600 poor Black sharecroppers in Macon County, Alabama, 399 with syphilis and 201 without the disease. There is no evidence the researchers ever obtained informed consent from the patients. Instead, participants were told they were being treated for "bad blood," a term widely understood by the Black population to include several health issues, including syphilis.

The men participating in the study received free medical exams, free meals, and burial insurance. After funding was lost for treatment, someone made the decision to continue the study, but those who were infected were never told they had the disease and never received treatment. At the beginning of the study, to determine which participants had the disease, spinal taps were conducted, but the patients were not told the purpose of the spinal taps. They were simply told it was a "special free treatment." It has been conjectured that researchers continued the study without syphilis treatment simply because they wanted to learn about progression of the disease in the body to the very end, until death.

The study was supposed to last only 6 months, but it continued for 40 years. Thousands of people participating in the study died of syphilis. Penicillin became widely accepted as a course of treatment in 1947, but those in the study who had the disease were never given penicillin. It wasn't until 1972 that Peter Buxtun, a social worker and epidemiologist working for the U.S. Public Health Service, discovered the truth about the program. Buxtun had been born and raised in Prague, Czechoslovakia. He was stunned to learn an experiment similar to the Nazis' human experimentation in concentration camps was going on in the United States. He leaked his findings to a reporter after several attempts to get the Public Health Service to stop the experiment.

As a result of Buxtun's leak to the press, congressional subcommittee meetings were held in early 1973 by Senator Edward Kennedy. The subcommittee found that the men had agreed to participate, but they had been misled. None of the participants were given all the information necessary to constitute informed consent, and none were ever given the option to quit the study. The panel advised stopping the study immediately, and in the Summer of 1973 a class action lawsuit was filed on behalf of study participants and their families. The U.S. government, as a part of a $10 million out-of-court settlement, provided lifetime medical benefits and burial services to all living participants and their families. The last participant died in January 2004, and the last widow receiving benefits died in 2009.

The history of the Tuskegee study is well-known among American Blacks. In fact, it is still due to accounts of this "human experimentation" that many Black patients say they wait as long as they can to seek medical care. They still distrust the system. Many Blacks will seek care only from Black health practitioners.

The Tuskegee syphilis study has been referred to as "arguably the most infamous biomedical research study in U.S. history" (Katz, et al., 2006). It's almost hard to believe it happened. The U.S. Public Health Service technically took responsibility for the misappropriations of the program, but institutions are made of people. As with the case of Henrietta Lacks, we have to ask how the decisions came about that led to this horrible situation. For our purposes, it's not a matter of blame—it's a matter of wanting to understand what happened within the hearts and minds of the individuals who made the decisions. The study of this type of motivation and behavior is what we call social science research.

Were the people who designed the Tuskegee program and continued the study even after funding was pulled aware of the ultimate consequences for participants—pain, suffering, and ultimately death? If so, why was that okay with them? If they were not aware of the gravity of these consequences, what was blocking their understanding? Does it have anything to do with race or the fact that the sharecroppers were poor? Would a program such as this ever have been put into place for a study of well-to-do White males with syphilis in the 1950s?

For the government, legal and financial consequences were the ultimate result of Tuskegee. Did those who initially made the decisions realize they were risking legal consequences? Or was there something within their personalities or personal experiences that allowed them to justify their actions, remain blind to that possibility, and continue conducting the examinations?

It's easy to imagine medical practitioners in those days, hungry for knowledge, desperately looking for human subjects to help them understand disease and find cures. Perhaps, by default, they gravitated toward citizens on the lowest rung of society. Perhaps they justified their actions with the thought that many millions of lives ultimately could be saved. Were those the same kinds of thoughts the doctors had about Henrietta Lacks' immortal tissues?

Human beings, for what they have believed to be good causes, have been willing to compromise compassion and ethics. It's unfathomable today to think that people could not have seen what was wrong with the Tuskegee study. Then again, why did people believe not long ago that it was okay to use experimental drugs on homeless people as long as we paid them?

Now let's take this examination of the people involved in the Tuskegee program one step further. After the program was dismantled and the lawsuit resolved, one wonders what those early decision makers were thinking. Did they suddenly understand the seriousness of their actions? Did they feel remorse, or were they still blind to the pain of the study participants and the unjustness of the program? Again, we aren't looking to blame. We simply are trying to understand what led to the decisions, so we can determine for the sake of argument what needs to be done to keep such terrible things from happening in the future.

One last question: Is it possible for those who are blind to the pain they have caused to examine themselves and understand what has gone wrong within themselves? Is it possible for them to change? Is it possible for any of us to change?

Questions

1. Have you encountered a cultural practice or tradition that at first seemed strange, but upon reflection was actually similar to your own? For example, hijabs worn by Muslim women could be seem similar to headwear of Christian nuns.
2. Think back to the scenario of being displaced in Mexico and having a family member in need of health care. What would be your expectations of the health care providers? What would be your response if those expectations were not met?
3. Have you ever felt afraid to seek help from people who are supposed to be helping/protecting you (e.g., police, doctors, firefighters, etc.)? If yes, where did that unease come from?

4

Memories of Pain

Flowers every night
Blossom in the sky;
Peace in the Infinite;
At peace am I.

—A. J. Arbery

My dad had a huge scar on the side of his face under his chin and down a part of his neck and shoulder. I don't remember the exact story, but I know he was burned accidentally with hot water. As a small girl, I was curious about it. I talked about the scar with him unabashedly, unburdened by worries that I might hurt his feelings. He knew I loved him, so he wasn't suspicious of my childlike assessment of his scar. I matter-of-factly told him the bumpy, pink skin looked like an egg-and-tomato omelet—a delicious breakfast dish loved by southern Iranians.

When he heard my description, he laughed. And then, I assume because he had felt the pain of other people's judgment of his scar, he used our conversation as a teaching moment. When people looked at his scar, he explained, they would try to guess what had happened but rarely were

Becoming Inclusive, pages 35–47
Copyright © 2021 by Information Age Publishing
All rights of reproduction in any form reserved.

able to guess. "You can't tell anything about people from the way they look," he said to me.

My dad's scar gave him both a curse and a gift that many people experience when they suffer from outward disabilities or disfigurements: The curse of exposure to judgment and the gift of adaptability—the ability to overcome hurt and help others manage their fear of the unknown.

My dad, as a result of adaptation to life with a scar on his face, had developed emotional strength. He was always understanding in the face of the quick judgments people would make about him when they saw the scar. No, he was not damaged mentally. No, he was not in pain. No, he had not been the victim of a crime.

My dad was resilient and full of hope when he could have been bitter and angry. No setback stopped him. He loved life and performed well at his job. He was devoted to his family. This was the focus he used to fuel his life, not worries or anger or resentfulness. This positive attitude made him mentally strong and empathetic, which are good qualities to possess when you work in human resources. Or when you want to teach your children to be strong and empathetic like you.

*   *   *

On November 4, 1979, a group of Iranian students attacked the U.S. Embassy in Tehran and took more than 60 people hostage. The news was filled with conjecture about the reasons this had happened. Some believed it was because then-President Jimmy Carter had allowed Iran's ousted king, Mohammad Reza Shah Pahlavi, to come to the United States for cancer treatment. Others believed it was far more than that—a dramatic way for the revolutionaries to declare a break with Iran's past and build momentum for a new Iran free from influences of the West.

Much can be said about the reasons for this tragic event. Perhaps it really began decades before, a result of Iran's desire to nationalize the country's oil, or maybe it stemmed from the CIA's intervention and overthrow of the government in the 1950s in order to maintain Western interests in Iranian oil. Analyzing and speculating about the actions and motivations behind the "Iranian Crisis," as it came to be known, is beyond the purpose of this book. Suffice it to say the crisis paved the way for the new Islamic Republic of Iran and for the Ayatollah Khomeini as its supreme leader. And it was the beginning of the broken relationship between Iran and the United States.

During that time, there was a mass exodus of Iranians to various parts of the world. It is said by the mid-2010s, two-thirds of Iranians were in their 30s or younger, while only one-third were over the age of 70. Iranians who then were between 30 and 70 years of age had left the country in the late 1970s and 1980s or were killed during the Iran/Iraq war of the 1980s. In the United States, the majority of emigrating Iranians chose southern California as their new home.

Because of the Iran hostage crisis of 1979, many people in the United States became leery of Iranians. For some it was the first time they had heard of Iran. Most literally knew nothing about the country and its people other than the horrible stories they were seeing on the news, and many Americans became angry and fearful of Iran. In the absence of meaningful in-person contact with the people of any culture, a person's brain has nothing to challenge the information it is receiving from media and other sources, and so it accepts new information (in this case, obtained mostly via news) as the way "everyone is."

I believe the workings of the human brain played an important role in the way Americans felt about Iran and Iranian immigrants after the 1970s crisis. As human beings, we are born with a need to self-protect. This becomes incredibly evident during times of perceived danger. Neuroscientists and social psychologists call the part of the brain that automatically engages at such times the "fight or flight" center of the brain or the Reptilian Brain. Thanks to research in neuroscience, we also know human beings connect to people like themselves and tend to be naturally mistrustful of people different from themselves—unless they have worked hard to develop neural pathways that lead their brains to different conclusions.

I can imagine the workings of some American brains following the Iranian Crisis. During times of crisis, the empathy center of the brain likely literally shuts down and mental vision becomes narrow. The ability to think critically (a function of the neocortex) is diminished. This happens because the brain needs to make quick life-and-death decisions. The need to attack is heightened and the desire for control increases. These were crucial functions of the brain for our ancestors in prehistoric times as they fled from wild animals. While most of us no longer have to outrun predatory animals, we do have a use for feeling this fight-or-flight emotion when we see an oncoming car or when our 2-year-old is about to jump into a pool.

At those times, we need this primitive part of our brain to do exactly what it is designed to do. At other times, such as when there is simply a lack of adequate information, which is no real danger to us, we need to recognize how to manage our primitive emotions—to control the impulses of our brain.

*   *   *

When the American hostages were taken in Iran in 1979, I was in my room within the girls' dormitory at Central Florida Academy and had no idea what was going on. None of us did. You have to remember, it was a time before we had access to 24/7 news. We didn't hear the news about Iran until some of us listened to newscasts the next morning. One of our classmates came to the dorm and told us Iranian students had attacked the American embassy. At first, we didn't know hostages had been taken—the story unfolded slowly in the news through an extended period. Many Americans watched reports after each segment of the nightly news. In fact, this nightly update on the Iranian Crisis gave birth to what is now the television news show *Night Line*.

As teenagers, we were unsure what to think about this horrible event in our home country. At first, we didn't think about what it meant for our families. The incident had taken place in Tehran, hundreds of miles from my family's home on Kharg Island, or from Masjed Soleyman and Ahwaz where most of our relatives lived at that time. But as the Iranian students talked, we began to worry about our loved ones across the sea. We all began receiving calls from our families, and each time a call was taken the news spread quickly. Some of the students were from Tehran. Bits of information were passed from person to person throughout the school when we heard someone's family member had been detained or another person's family was trying hard to leave the country. I remember a deep fear settling into my belly as I became more and more afraid for my family—and my fear worsened when the war began with Iraq. We were afraid of what might happen both in Iran and in Florida. What would this mean for our future?

This added a new dimension to the personal ridicule and humiliation that had entered my life beginning in 1976. Before the hostage crisis, I had been mocked mostly because I was generally different from the insecure British and American teenagers who felt threatened by all of the unknowns associated with me. They also didn't like that I wasn't willing to change to suit them. After the crisis, this fear of unknowns gained a new definition and focus. The events in Iran deepened the suspicion of some people and, for some, turned their disdain to hatred. Some of the newer Iranian students, including me, my brothers, and friends who had just arrived at the academy a few months earlier, felt this hatred and fear coming our way even from fellow students.

As the hostage crisis continued, the expressions of fear toward me and my fellow Iranians at the academy became more public. There were instances of microaggression almost daily. People protested, yelling in the streets and carrying signs that said, "Camel Jockeys go home." I remember the first time a friend called me a Camel Jockey. She laughed and then said, "I'm just kidding, you know that, right?" Another friend's father called me Sand Nigger and followed it with, "But you are the prettiest Sand Nigger I know." These are small things that in and of themselves are not a big deal, but a hundred small acts of aggression toward one person build up and damage the psyche.

When my brothers and I talked with our parents, they told us everything was fine. They didn't want us to worry. Many years later, I found out they were *not fine* at that time. They had been evacuated in the middle of the night to Abadan, then later to Tehran, because Iraq had attacked Kharg Island.

One day, shortly after the hostages were taken in Iran, school officials gathered all Iranian students at the school and told us they were required by the U.S. government to bring us to the Orlando International Airport.

I still don't know what specifics immigration officials at the airport were looking for. They examined our official papers and asked questions about why we had come to the United States and how our families were employed in Iran. I believe some students were detained and sent back to Iran. The rest of us were driven back to school on the bus and told we could stay there as long as we continued our education.

The Ku Klux Klan (KKK) made it known we weren't welcome. I knew nothing about the organization until that time, although we were in the heart of KKK country. My first clue was my dorm mom, Mrs. Anderson's, refusal to allow me to go to a barbecue with a boy whose father was a leader in the KKK. "You'll become the barbecue," she joked, with enough of a serious note that I relented.

After the hostages were taken in Iran, the KKK looked for ways to make their opinion of us known. For example, during a hayrack ride for students at our school, we heard gunshots and the sponsors instantly took us back to the dorm. The rumor was that the KKK was shooting our way because they knew there were Iranians at the school. If it was them, I have to assume they were only trying to scare us. I don't think I was aware enough of what was happening to be as terrified as I maybe should have been. I remember thinking, "They don't even know me. How can they hate me?"

Some of the non-Iranian students, teachers, and local citizens would talk about the hostage situation in ways that made us feel unwelcome and afraid. One day, I went shopping with a group of Iranian students at

Altamonte Springs Mall in Orlando. One of the store employees at the mall began chatting with us. She seemed nice, and it felt good to have a normal conversation with a friendly member of the community. When she asked where we were from, one of my friends said, "Iran." We instantly were asked to leave, politely but firmly thrown out of the store and told never to come back. We were in shock and disbelief.

This experience wasn't an isolated incident. At that time, stores were selling dartboards and T-shirts with "Death to the Ayatollah" on them. People were singing, "Bomb, Bomb, Bomb—Bomb, Bomb Iran" to the Beach Boys' tune, "Barbara Ann." We heard and read jokes about Iranians being Ragheads. On more than one occasion, I was told, "Go home! You don't belong here."

What could I do? I couldn't change where I had been born. I couldn't change who my parents were. Didn't they understand that the political situation in Iran had nothing to do with my teenage world at the academy? I felt embarrassed to be Iranian, but a part of me wanted them to know about the beautiful parts of life in Iran—the hot summer nights in the village on the hill, the cozy house on Kharg Island and the loving embrace of my cousins and grandparents. Not every Iranian hated Americans. Not every Iranian was a terrorist. We had lives remarkably similar to theirs when I had lived in Iran.

In my mind, there was only one thing I could do: not admit to being Iranian. It was a matter of emotional survival. When people asked me where I was from, I began by asking them, "Where do I look like I'm from?" People would guess all kinds of places. Mostly Mexico, sometimes Greece. My typical response was, "You are so smart!" or "How did you guess?" This was a measure of protection I used for many years after the hostage crisis had cooled. To this day, if I meet someone new and they have openly voiced disdain for people from the Middle East, I will not mention my place of birth. It makes me sad, and I wish it wasn't so.

* * *

Mrs. Anderson was faithful to her promise to my mother and father. She left a piece of fresh fruit on my pillow every day. Instead of teaching me how to do my laundry, which she believed would add to my stress, she took my laundry home with her and returned it clean. She saw my sorrow and sadness in the days, weeks, and months after my parents left and wanted me to know she cared.

The United States seemed very strange to me and confusing in many ways. Mrs. Anderson took me to my first American football game. "Why are they so puffed up?" I asked her. I had thought they were going to play soccer, because in Iran we called soccer "football." My first Thanksgiving and Christmas breaks were spent in the Andersons' home, because Mrs. Anderson wanted me to see how "real" Americans celebrated the holidays.

Because of her words and actions, I could tell Mrs. Anderson truly was concerned about what happened to me. The day the authorities gathered us up and loaded us onto the bus after the hostages were taken in Iran, she was as upset as we were. She grabbed her son Andy, who was 5 years older than me and happened to be visiting his mom that afternoon, and said, "He'll marry you if he has to, to keep you here!"

I don't know what life would have been like at that time without Mrs. Anderson watching over me. Even though I missed my parents and was afraid of what might happen, everything was a little better because her empathy, attention, and communication made me feel a little more anchored in this strange land.

I settled into a routine and the months began passing more easily. I graduated from high school 8 days after my 16th birthday. I had been accepted to several colleges throughout the United States, but I didn't want to leave the security and comfort of my new home. I decided to stay in Sorrento and go to the community college there, so I would be close to the Andersons. When it became difficult for my parents to send money out of Iran, I moved in with the Andersons. I worked hard at school. Then, when I was almost finished with my associate's degree, my mother and 18-month-old sister Helena finally were able to move to the United States. My sister had been born in August of 1980, almost a year after my parents dropped us off at the boarding school. My mom and Helena were given visas because my younger brother and I were finished with high school but still minors,

My life was about to change—again.

* * *

The process of migration is difficult. When an organization is moving employees (expatriates) to another country, the company works hard to help them acculturate (adapt) to the new country. Even with support, displaced workers often experience months of sadness, loneliness, and trouble adjusting.

Immigrants don't usually receive such support from an organization, so the distressing feelings are exacerbated. Refugees, who are forced to flee their homeland to find safety and security, experience "exasperation on steroids!" My brothers and I were a little bit of both—part immigrant and part refugee. Our discomfort was further magnified because we were so young and had no family with us.

The adaptation process happens slowly, and if the process is to be as effective as possible a great deal of support is needed for a person going through the transition. It's difficult to understand if you haven't experienced this. A big hole is created when you leave your home country. You feel disoriented in the new culture and uncertain how to handle even small daily habits, which often vary from country to country. An immigrant can experience a rollercoaster of emotion: the highs and excitement of experiencing new things and of having made a decision and following through, then the lows of homesickness and frustration with new rules.

A refugee experiences mostly lows, including sorrow and fear, but there are a few highs, too: the relief of escaping a dangerous situation and the excitement of seeing new places. Both immigrants and refugees can have delayed reactions to all the changes and the first few months in a new country are filled with head-spinning new sensory input.

For nonimmigrants who want to understand, it might help to think about a time when you moved from one city to another. Imagine you can't go back to your city, because war has broken out there, as in the Canadian/ American scenario earlier in this book. Your family members are still in your home city. In the new city, you have to learn a new language, work, and go to school, all at the same time. To make matters worse, you don't know if you will be allowed to stay in this new place. Can you feel the emotions—all of the emotions? Fear, anger, confusion, sorrow, excitement, determination. What else might you feel?

Once you've imagined this uncomfortable and distressing situation, then imagine people saying you aren't doing anything right just because you aren't doing things like they do. Imagine people making fun of your language or getting frustrated with you when you don't know how to behave properly at the grocery store or the gas station in your new home. How would you cope?

We know from years of psychological research that this process of adapting to a new place is extremely difficult. The older the person, the longer it takes to learn a new language. The younger the person, the more they need to feel safe and protected.

There are different types of adaptation. Sometimes it is forced assimilation (the most damaging type). Sometimes, adaptation involves acculturation, which means it involves a personal decision (the least damaging type). With assimilation, the adapting person is told, "Who you were is not good enough to be where you are." With acculturation, the person says to himself or herself, "This is a different place, and I want to figure out how to adapt."

In my own life, I began in assimilation and the older I became the closer I moved to acculturation. I know the difference well.

Assimilation says, "I can't say your name. Can I call you Tom, Sally, or John? Acculturation says, "People seem to be having difficulty saying my name. I wonder how I can shorten it, or modify it to make it easier on them?"

Assimilation says, "If you don't know our language, you must be stupid or lazy." Acculturation says, "I understand how long it takes to learn a language, but I'm determined to become proficient no matter how long it takes me."

The person, organization, or community forcing assimilation usually wants changes to happen right now in expatriates, immigrants, and refugees. (Think microwave society.)

The person, organization, or community helping new friends acculturate are patient. They are willing to nudge when necessary and be the scaffolding when necessary. (Think crockpot society.)

Here's the crux of it all: Assimilation most often leads to resistance, anger, and disconnection. Acculturation leads to gradual, healthy adaptation. Most of us would rather acculturate when we move to a new country. But many people want strangers coming into their countries to assimilate.

* * *

I loved my mom and was excited to have her nearby again. But my time in the United States had changed me. It was a necessary change. To survive in my isolation within the American world, I had to become American, at least to some degree. In my formative teenage years, I took on American characteristics by choice and created the life of an American girl. I learned how to do it with Mrs. Anderson's help, as well as by watching and imitating other teenagers around me.

I sometimes wonder if I would have changed as much if the hostage crisis in Iran hadn't happened at such a formative time in my life. As a sensitive teenager, it was so important to be accepted. I was willing to do what was necessary to avoid feeling different and avoid some people's contempt. That's why I would allow people to guess where I was from instead of telling them I was Iranian.

When I moved in with my mom and sister in St. Petersburg, Florida, I realized we had both changed drastically. Mom wanted what we'd had in England, but her time in Iran had turned her into a "strong Iranian–Muslim woman": modest, quiet, and focused on education for her children at all costs. By contrast, I had become an active, independent 17-year-old "Americanized" girl. I went to school at the University of South Florida in the Fall of 1982, as Mom expected me to do, but we began to argue about many things. When cultures collide, it is painful for all the people involved. When the collision is with family, the pain goes even deeper.

One of the biggest problems was that our work ethic was now different. I valued my education, but I had learned how to have fun. My mother, who had become even more conservative, felt that any distraction from education had to be removed. She wanted me to spend 16 hours a day studying and 8 hours sleeping, and nothing else. She was an introvert who was happy being at home by herself, but I was an extrovert who needed to be with people. I learned by talking and doing, as opposed to my mom, who learned by reading and writing. I think she believed, because of the way I had changed, that I was not willing to comply with any of the rules she set in her role as my mom.

My mom was horrified that I had a boyfriend—it was nothing serious, but to her he was a threat to my education. She began to check up on me, in my mind violating my right to privacy. I didn't believe my association with the people of America detracted from my education. On the contrary, I believed it enriched my education. I loved being around people from all parts of the world and learning from them. I thought socializing was an education in itself. I enjoyed talking with the Andersons on the phone, for example, and getting updates about the people who had become my surrogate family.

I know my mom was simply reinforcing what she felt was best for me, but I felt I was being forced into a mold I no longer fit. When I came home from school, I felt like a caged animal, miles away from everything familiar to me. Today, with children of my own, I look back on this time with greater understanding. My mom was desperate to "protect" me. I was desperate to live my own life.

So I escaped.

I ran away and lived with my friends and former roommates from Florida Central Academy, Farah and Sophia. They lived in Clearwater, about 40 miles from the university, but I didn't care how far away it was from school or my mother. My independence was worth the hardships this brought to my life. I hitchhiked to college from the girls' apartment 3 days a week and worked at a McDonalds® restaurant near where we lived. We were all so broke, some days we had only 1 meal to eat—and that was sometimes food McDonalds was throwing away.

In one important way, I did not stray from my parents' wishes. They had already paid for my schooling, so I refused to quit. My mother and sister had waited in line with me for hours during registration at the University of South Florida. Although I didn't want to live with them, I couldn't bear the thought of quitting when my parents had sacrificed so much for my education.

When the semester was finished, I had a choice. Stay where I was, move in with my mother again, or move back to the Andersons, 3 hours away. I chose the Andersons. I wanted to be free to make my own decisions and go to college without feeling as though I was always being watched. I know my mom felt betrayed, and I am sorry now to have caused her that pain.

To earn money for tuition, I began working at another McDonalds with Mrs. Andersons' daughter, Laura. I consider Laura my American sister. On our first day, when we walked into the new-employee orientation, the first thing I saw was the behind of a bent-over young man who was preparing a video for our session. I liked what I saw and whispered to Laura, "That's the butt I'm going to marry." It was a joke, but it wasn't long before I began dating Scott Fagan.

I buckled down to work and saved money for school. I had 9 months to save for the fall semester. Then, one day, I received a letter demanding my appearance at an immigration hearing. My mother had given the U.S. immigration office my name and address at the Andersons and had told immigration officers that I was working illegally. I was furious and heart-broken at the time. Today, I know my mother's belief that I was ruining my life had been so strong that she decided the best way to protect me was to force me back to Iran.

"What can they do?" Scott asked as we talked about it on the phone.

"They can deport me," I said matter-of-factly.

"I won't let them do it," he said.

"What are you going to do, marry me?" I asked, laughing. And to my surprise he said that is exactly what he would do. I reminded him he was only 17 and still in high school. And he would be leaving to fulfill orders for the U.S. Navy a month after graduation.

"We are too young," I said, serious now, "and I don't want you to marry me because you feel sorry for me." I thought to myself, I've heard this before when Mrs. Anderson said Andy would marry me. I thought this was the same kind of thing—an expression of love and concern, but not a serious proposal. Scott insisted he did not feel sorry for me. He professed his love and said he couldn't bear the thought of me going back to Iran.

The next day I received a letter beautifully written by Scott asking me to marry him. He said he didn't care how young we were and believed we could make it if we tried. I loved him, too, so I said yes. Our plan was to get married the following December when he completed boot camp and telecommunications school. I would go back to school wherever we landed after that.

Finally, I felt at peace with my life.

As the future wife of a U.S. sailor, I knew where I belonged. With him. The Andersons were not happy with my decision, but they were moving to Dallas anyway and knew I would have to find another place to live if I wanted to stay in Florida. They gave me a car and some money, and I moved in with a fellow McDonalds employee—a single mother of 2 children.

Scott took me to the Immigration hearing in June. As my fiancé, he was allowed to go into the hearing with me. The judge was not sympathetic. In spite of our engagement, which he may have seen as an attempt to circumvent the law, he told me if I didn't leave voluntarily by September, I would be deported and not allowed to come back anytime soon—if ever. Scott and I were shocked. Both of us were silent on the drive home, each of us lost in our thoughts.

The next day, Scott showed up at my door. He had talked with his parents. They would sign for him, since he was under the legally marriageable age, which had meant we could get married before he left for boot camp on July 21st. I couldn't believe it. I felt so loved and cared for. I couldn't wait to be Mrs. Scott Fagan. I knew it would not be a popular decision with some of the people in my life, but I was at peace with it. I began to feel excited—as any young bride should feel.

We set the date for a wedding: July 8, 1983, only 3 weeks away. My friends Farah and Sophia thought I was crazy to marry an American without my parents' permission. My friends at work thought I was pregnant. I wasn't. In fact, we waited several years to have children to prove it. Louise Anderson expressed her worry. She convinced a friend to come to McDonalds and try to talk me out of it. She didn't want me to give up on my parents' dream for my life and really believed I was marrying Scott just to get a green card. Much later, I found out Scott's parents also believed our marriage was simply a way for me to get a green card, but they wanted to support their son in his effort to help me, and they knew we could get a divorce afterwards and be done with it.

My friend Farah told my older brother about the wedding, and he told my parents. It is not exaggerating to say they were devastated by this news. It was not the future they had wanted for me for so long. At the time, young and in love, I didn't understand. But I do now. I probably would feel the same in their shoes. At that time, though, as a bride-to-be full of excitement and confidence in my future, I couldn't understand their displeasure.

Honestly, I didn't feel I *was being forced* to marry Scott to stay in the United States. I knew my father had the connections to keep me in the country if I wanted or needed him to. But I believed then, and have always believed, that God intended for Scott and me to be together. Even though we were different in many ways, including the ways we were raised, we were instinctively drawn to each other—as opposites often are. On a deeper level, we felt a strong emotional connection to one another and a sense of commitment. We understood each other, were deeply in love, and believed this was the right thing to do.

Our decision would mean some major changes in Scott's life. As the husband of a non-U.S. citizen, especially an Iranian citizen, he couldn't be in telecommunications, because it required a security clearance. So, he switched careers and became an engineman (diesel mechanic). In my mind, his decision about this proved he really loved me. With a new life rising up to embrace me, the anguish I had felt during my first years at the academy began to fade, the Iranian crisis suddenly seemed light years away, and I felt much of my pain being overshadowed by happiness.

Questions

1. What is your gut reaction when you hear about protesters in another country? Why do you think you respond this way?
2. We have all endured challenging times in our lives. How have you allowed those challenging times to make you stronger? Better? Wiser? More resilient? More purposeful? How are you using the challenging times in your life to help others grow?
3. Think about a time you had a strong disagreement with a family member. Did you ever consider why they may hold the belief that you're disagreeing on? Where may that belief have come from and what in your life has caused you to differ from this belief?

$$5$$

Shifting Perceptions

From the arrival of spring and the passing of yesterday,
the pages of our lives keep passing away.

—K. Amouzgar

As the day of our wedding approached, I was happier than I had ever remembered feeling. We were so poor, we had to make do with what we had, but everything was going wonderfully under the circumstances. I would wear the dress I had worn to Scott's high school prom. We would be married at his parent's church, and the Reverend Vanus Smith would preside over the ceremony. Everything happened so quickly. Scott bought a suit from the Salvation Army, then two silver wedding bands at the flea market. We went together to get our blood test and apply for the marriage license. We sent no invitations; we would have only about ten people with us at the wedding.

The afternoon before the wedding, I was at home shaving my legs. The phone rang and I left the shower, one leg shaved and one unshaved, to answer it. A coworker at McDonald's was calling to tell me a man was there asking for me. The man said he was my father and claimed he wouldn't

Becoming Inclusive, pages 49–62
Copyright © 2021 by Information Age Publishing
All rights of reproduction in any form reserved.

leave until he talked with me. I was so anxious and excited—I hadn't known my dad was in the United States. I remember smiling the minute I heard his voice on the phone.

"I heard you were getting married and I want to talk to you," he said. All of a sudden, a little dread was mixed with the excitement, but I told him I would meet him. I quickly finished shaving, dressed, and drove to McDonald's. When I walked in, I saw not only my dad, but also my older brother, my little sister, and my friend Farah. While Farah and my brother Mehrdad took my little sister to the playground, Dad and I sat in one of the booths at the back of the restaurant and talked for a long time.

He told me I didn't have to get married, because he would contact the judge and talk to him. He would take care of everything. I told him I really loved Scott and really did want to be his wife. I could see he was sad, and I understood. It was not his dream that I would get married at 18. He wanted me to go to school and reminded me that I had promised him I would become a doctor and help save people's lives.

"You will be poor," my dad said, stating the obvious. "It was not my goal to bring my kids to America, only to have them live without money and not go to school. You know we have sacrificed much to bring you here because we wanted an excellent education for you."

"I know, dad," I said, acting as grown up as I could for an 18-year-old who was about to marry a 17-year-old. "I respect that. I have not forgotten my promise, and I will do my best to make sure your sacrifices were not in vain. But I have found my path—if only you could see that I can finally touch the happiness you have wanted for me. This is my home now, Agha. Please understand."

In the end, he did understand—or he said he did, for my sake. Was it because he knew he had no choice? Maybe. Parents do that sometimes, because they don't want to irreparably destroy the bond between themselves and their children. I believe it was the same reason Scott's parents had agreed to our marriage. We have to let go of our children. And it's never easy, no matter what country we are in.

* * *

In the book *Thinking Fast and Slow,* Daniel Kahneman (2011) does a great job of helping the reader understand the two systems of the brain: the fast system (unconscious, automatic, associative, intuitive, judgmental), which he calls the "System 1 brain," and the slow system (conscious, deliberate, logical, rational, inclusive) which he calls the "System 2 brain." In unpacking

Kahneman's research, we see that thoughts, beliefs, and attitudes can move from the slow System 2 brain to the fast System 1 brain with training.

Understanding this distinction gives us hope that humanity is capable of using the conscious brain to think deliberately and move beyond our biases (the ways our brains sort good and evil) to recognizing the impact and limitations of those biases. If, however, you've had no opportunity to build adequate pathways in the conscious brain, you might hear and understand and accept me even if I am different from you but when you leave my presence you go back to being navigated by your biases in the fully developed pathways in your unconscious brain where your deepest beliefs have been forged and are now embedded. That is also where your thoughts will land in times of crisis or stress or perceived threat.

Our System 2 brain is the last part of our brain to develop. It has to be exercised like our physical body to grow and develop. One of the greatest arguments for liberal arts in higher education is that it can help develop the System 2 brain, because in this course of study, students learn to synthesize information. When the System 2 brain is exercised through those "general education" courses, there is a greater likelihood a person will be able to access the System 2 brain intentionally when needed. I have seen this in the courses I teach, in the clients I have worked with, and in the research I have conducted.

The dean of students at a health sciences college told me nurses who complete a liberal arts undergraduate degree and then choose to become nurses tend to perform better in nursing skills courses. She said this is because the purpose of the nursing skills courses is to synthesize everything the student learned in "technical" classes (anatomy and physiology, pharmacology, chemistry, medical terminology, etc.) and then apply that knowledge to caring for patients (using critical thinking, ethical judgement, problem solving, and decision-making). To do this, they can use the skill of synthesizing information they learned through their liberal arts degree.

A chief of police told me his officers who have liberal arts education tend to do better at problem solving and are less likely to make poor decisions. That is not to say that a technical education isn't valid or should be eliminated from our education system. However, this example points out that for higher order thinking, which requires System 2 of the brain to be online, we must endeavor to include lessons that challenge the brain and help it grow and develop.

Physical exercise, to be effective, must first tear down old tissue and make room for new tissue to grow, and that's what makes a person physically stronger. Similarly, with the brain, to break down the old way of thinking and grow a new way of thinking, we have to exercise our brains. Without developing this ability, when we perceive a threat, our System 2 brain is the first to go offline, which allows the stronger, more prominent, unconscious System 1 brain to take over, and that's normally where judgmental fears take over and block inclusive abilities and thoughts.

Once a person has worked intentionally to forge new pathways in the neocortex it will be easier for that individual to shift perspective and to objectively evaluate their beliefs when they perceive threats.

I'm not a medical scientist, so I can only wonder at the thousands of details involved in this mechanism of the brain. But this information does raise many questions related to diversity, inclusion, and intercultural agility. If it's true that establishment of pathways in the neocortex allows people to become more accepting of others, how do those pathways get there? One thought that crosses my mind is ongoing authentic and positive interactions with those different from us combined with objective and intentional self-reflection regarding the interaction.

I believe seeking to have positive and authentic interactions with those different from us creates synapses in the neocortex that allow empathy and understanding to become a fundamental part of our approach to differences. That would certainly explain why Scott was able to see past the differences between us—even in a difficult time, when people like me were feared and denigrated. It certainly would explain why my father, who had spent a lifetime preparing me and my brothers for leadership in Iran, could turn on a dime and suddenly support my marriage, which he must have known would keep me from remaining a citizen of our home country forever.

Think about people you know who are very different from one another, but who support or even love each other. It's likely they have developed a high capacity for empathy that helps them see past each other's differences. I believe when a person sits with their own fears, doubts, and biases in such a way that they can recognize those in others, it develops the capacity for empathy. I have seen this in my work as a diversity professional. The greater the level of empathy a person has, the more likely the person is able to understand someone who's different from them.

In my experience, hardship has the potential to develop empathy. In Scott's case, for example, I believe hardships in his early life transformed him into a very mature and empathetic human being. Some refugees and immigrants I've worked with have struggled so much to adapt to new places but have a great capacity for empathizing with others, while other refugees and immigrants who have had similar struggles have very little empathy and are filled with bitterness and anger.

The outcome of hardship is not always positive. It's not uncommon for people who have been hated to develop hatred. In fact, in the field of criminal psychology it is believed that serial murderers have not developed the part of the brain responsible for empathy. What's the difference? What makes one person choose hate, while another is able to empathize, understand, and interact positively with those who are different?

Perhaps, as you are reading this book you can think of people in your life who are finding it difficult to accept others who are different. The reasons this happens are complex, ranging from the biological and political to the psychological and spiritual. To connect authentically with one's own experiences and from there build a mental bridge to the experiences of others is the process of developing empathy and a new mindset. The new mindset gives us the ability to shift perspective and see the world not just through the lens of our own experience, but the experiences of others, too.

*   *   *

I would have loved my dad no matter what, but I loved and respected him all the more because he heard me that day at McDonald's, treated me as an adult and allowed me to make my own decision. Until then, I had felt that no one heard me. My conversations with the people in my life had always centered around *their* views of me and *their* hopes for me. No one really had ever stopped to ask what I wanted, who I was, or what was meaningful to me. I felt freedom in this feeling and in the joy and wonder of my wedding day.

I also loved my dad because he went everywhere in a suit. He was already dressed to walk me down the aisle and that is what he did in spite of his feelings. Our wedding was simple. I carried a silk bouquet from a friend's wedding a few weeks before. We served a homemade Duncan Hines® cake at our very small reception. The whole thing cost less than $75. We had no decorations, few photographs and a 1-night "honeymoon" thanks to Scott's stepdad Robert Bliss, who worked at Walt Disney World and gave us 2 tickets to Epcot Center for a day. No one thought we would make it as a married couple for 6 months, much less a lifetime.

Anytime I slow down long enough to remember that day, I am filled with a sense of the peace, strength, and confidence I felt with every step I took down that red carpeted aisle of the church. My father had honored me by walking me down the aisle in spite of his ambivalence. Scott honored me and showed true love by changing his profession, fitting into *my* life instead of insisting that I fit into his. I was humbled by this outpouring of respect and compassion. It made me determined to live up to the promises I had made.

A few months after our wedding, we went to visit my parents, sister, and brothers in Tampa, Florida. My dad took Scott aside and sat him down with his accounting books. He showed Scott all the money he had spent on his children and shared with him the sacrifices, dreams, and hopes he had for my future. He made Scott promise to do whatever it took to help me advance my education and love me unconditionally above everyone else. Scott promised him that. And he has kept that promise.

* * *

In July 1991, my father and little sister, who was then 11 years old, came to visit us in Virginia Beach, Virginia. We were living there because Scott was stationed aboard the USS Boulder. Dad would be staying with us for about a month, then planned to stop over in Detroit where my younger brother was completing his surgical residency. He would then travel back to California where my mom, sister, and older brother were living. It had been 6 years since I had last seen my dad. He had returned to Iran in 1985 and had been unable to get another visa to reenter the United States.

It had been almost two decades since my dad and I had spent more than a few days together—since my childhood, really. This time, there would be no make-believe tea parties. He could no longer pick me up and dance with me in his arms. This was real life, and I had so much to tell him to bring him up to speed with the bountiful life that had resulted from his guidance, even if it didn't match his goals for me, including the all-important education he had deeply sacrificed for. A part of me hoped he still thought of me as his *holoo koochooloo,* his little peach.

Scott and I and our sons, Jonathan, then 5 years old, and Alan, a little over a year old, went to pick up my dad and sister from the airport. As we stood with a loose crowd of people waiting for passengers, my mind was filled with tender images from my childhood: daffodil blossoms in the spring, our life in Masjed Soleyman, our home on Kharg Island, and our life in England. I cherished my childhood memories with my family and the country of my birth. I still wanted to please Agha. Would some of that old affection ever return to us?

Then my mind suddenly filled with a vision of the tanks in Iran that summer long ago—and I realized with the understanding of an adult what that must have meant to my dad. He must have been fearful and disappointed. How had he and my mom endured the uncertainty of those times? Did they have regrets, realizing it could be difficult for their children to return to Iran—suspecting the country would never be the same again? What had made it okay for them to live apart for the sake of my brothers and me? How had they overcome the many detours in their plans? Had they felt the same pain I had of being from a country that some Americans thought of as hostile and suspicious?

Standing there, watching planes touch down and take off at Norfolk airport, I asked myself for the umpteenth time: Had I made the right decision to marry Scott and stay in the United States? And then I answered myself for the umpteenth time: Of course I had. But now, with so much time having passed, I wondered if my father would agree.

The truth was, it hadn't been easy, and I had hardships of my own to share with my dear, precious Agha. After our wedding, I had become defined by yet another culture—the challenging culture of the military. A Navy wife is often lonely and removed from family, living in a new place, having to learn to navigate life on her own. For me, this kind of life hadn't been completely new. I just had not fully comprehended that being a Navy wife would involve living like that. My life became lonely once again. Once more, I was left to my own devices, this time while Scott served his country to care for his family. It wasn't that I didn't want him to have the career he desired. He already had given up so much for me. But living on my own while Scott was at sea brought back painful memories of the loneliness and unhappiness I had felt in England when I'd had to live without my father and especially at the boarding school in Florida when I had been isolated from both my parents and my siblings.

There were other sorrows, too—many normal life disappointments Scott and I had to face together. I had suffered two miscarriages. I had bounced from job to job because every time the Navy moved us, I had to find a new one. Our finances were a constant issue. We suffered together through the death of Scott's older 22-year-old brother who fell asleep at the wheel of his car, we worried about my dad's heart-related illnesses, and we faced other life crises. On top of all of that, Scott and I didn't always agree. The different upbringings gave us different ideas about how to raise our children, how to keep our house, how to spend money, and the role extended family should play in our decisions.

I found an interesting solution to navigating life as a Navy wife. I volunteered to be an Ombudsman for Scott's ship. That position kept me connected to him and the ship and it helped alleviate my pain, because I was helping other young wives and families face the challenges of adapting to life in a new place without the aid of family. It was really my first role in managing differences between people. I was 27 and felt I had more experience than most women twice my age.

When I look back, now I know much of my pain had to do with separation. I was separated from my family for years. I was separated from Scott when his ship was out to sea. I didn't realize then that all the moving and adjusting was taking a toll on my psyche. My lifelong motto has always been, "That which does not kill me makes me stronger." With every move, every separation, I dug in and worked hard to become stronger. I forced myself to stay positive. I pushed the pain aside. Little did I know the damage this "strong-arming" of myself would have on me. It would be decades before my body would force me to address that pain.

* * *

During dad's visit with us in Virginia Beach, Scott's ship went out to sea. He was gone most of the month Dad was there. I kept the boys out of daycare and left them in dad's care. I went to work each day in the human resources department of First Hospital Corporation (FHC), which owned 16 psychiatric and drug/alcohol rehab hospitals all over the country as well as one in Puerto Rico. One day, I showed my dad my resume and described to him what I did at work. He told me that much of what I was doing was similar to what he had done during his early career at the oil company.

When I came home from work each evening, we had hours to catch up and get to know one another again. It was amazing watching dad play with our boys as he had done with me when I was a girl. It was a strange feeling watching from the outside. I was happy the boys were getting to know him in some of the same ways I had. Wonderful memories of my childhood poured into my mind as I watched them playing, singing, telling stories— and hugging and kissing. Agha adored my precious children as much as he had adored me when I was little.

It was a healing time for me, a time I desperately wanted to last forever. My dad could see how happy I was in this life in spite of the struggles he knew Scott and I had faced. He shared his hopes, dreams, and disappointments with me during those hours and days together. Now that I was a parent myself, I was able to understand his decisions and actions anew through the eyes of a parent. He also gave me time to share my own hopes, dreams, and disappointments with him. He acknowledged that my life was now in America. "I want you to make this your homeland," he said to me one day as we walked in the park.

At last.

I could be at peace with that part of my journey. I could believe Agha was no longer in pain because of my actions. I could stop worrying that he disapproved. But I soon felt a nagging gap in my peace. In a way, his acceptance intensified my inner struggle. He had accepted me against all odds and to my surprise something was still missing.

Dad wasn't feeling well during his visit and took frequent naps. I could tell he was in pain, but he insisted on getting up each evening to cook Iranian food for us, because he knew I loved it. He worked through the pain and we were able to fit in some sightseeing while Scott was away. I took a few days off so we could drive up to Washington, DC with the kids. While there, in addition to visiting some of the country's most beloved monuments, dad renewed all of our passports at the Iranian Interest Section of the Pakistani Embassy (Iran has not had an embassy in the United States since 1979)— part of the reason he had come. I entertained the boys and my sister all day while he took care of it.

Afterward, he told me about an Iranian woman who had been in the embassy. She was trying to make arrangements to get her husband's body back to Iran. Dad was upset by her struggle. "I kept thinking, if something happens to me, just bury me here," he told me. "I want to be near my family." His words broke my heart. I know how much he loved his home country. I guess he loved us more. It was satisfying and unsettling at the same time. When exactly did he shift from thinking, "My kids will be going back to Iran" to "My kids will be staying in the United States"?

"You won't have to worry about where you will be buried for a long time," I told him. But I was wrong. The doctors later said he was probably having mini strokes during the time he was with us. I didn't know it at the time, but I did realize in my heart that the time he was spending with us was precious and rare.

As always, Dad had a suit with him, so I had asked him to sit with us for a family portrait. As we waited for the photographer, I studied my family— the people who meant everything to me. Scott was so very American, even though he was married to an Iranian and had half-Iranian children. Agha was so very Iranian, even though he now wanted to be buried in America. My sister, who had been in the United States since she was 18 months old and had lived most of her life in San Diego, was more American than Iranian. My children were American with both Caucasian and Persian blood running through their veins.

But what was I?

I had chosen America, but I didn't have the American blood and many Americans had at one time violently objected to my presence here.

I had chosen to remain here, but I loved what I remembered of my childhood in Iran—and I could not deny my heritage, nor did I want to. What did this mean? Was I American or Iranian?

* * *

Jose Antonio Vargas, journalist, filmmaker, and immigration rights activist, is the CEO of Define American, a "non-profit media and culture organization that seeks to elevate the conversation around immigration and citizenship in America." Define American is about humanizing immigration and changing the way immigrants are perceived. I believe it's also about helping immigrants feel safe and comfortable as the "friends, neighbors, classmates, colleagues and community members they already are"—as human beings who are accepted and welcomed, even if they are not documented, and given a reasonable pathway to citizenship.

Interestingly enough, the word "illegal" is inaccurate when referencing undocumented immigrants. As the organization's website indicates, "Being in the U.S. without proper documents is a civil offense, not a criminal one." Supreme Court Justice Anthony Kennedy has said, "As a general rule, it is not a crime for a movable alien to remain in the United States."

The Define American website includes many stories of undocumented immigrants in the United States "coming out" and telling their stories, including what it means to them to live in the United States and the contributions they make to the country. Ultimately, the goal of this movement is immigration reform, but I believe it is first about caring for and about each other as fellow residents of the same country and celebrating our differences instead of fearing, demeaning, and discounting people who are different from ourselves. In the context of a hopeful vision of the United States' future, isn't this what it means to be American?

* * *

Since the American revolution, immigrants have flooded into the United States, at some times at a more rapid rate than others. As technology improved and travel became easier, the people of many countries have expanded their knowledge and experience of places and peoples other than their own.

The Internet profoundly changed our world by instantly connecting people of all races and ethnicities. Years ago, I didn't have to hear whether others agreed or disagreed with me. Today, I see their opinions on social media every waking minute. I can get on a plane almost immediately and get to China if I want to—on the same day. If I have even a small business, I might have a customer in Russia I've never met, but who I speak to online every day. In a single neighborhood, people can have many different religions, values, views, and backgrounds. In all of these ways, the opportunity to meet and interact with people who are different from ourselves has exploded. We have and continue to rapidly become a global community, and it cannot be denied that much good has come from it.

Our increased exposure to one another has, however, also caused a great deal of pain and loss. If the transportation technology had not existed to allow my parents to bring me to the United States, I never would have experienced the agony of being labeled a Sand Nigger or the humiliation of hearing shots fired over my head, possibly courtesy of the KKK.

Although many good things are happening between people in modern times, human beings in general still seem to possess fundamental barriers to navigating differences of language, perception, values, norms, beliefs, life goals, and more. The pain of being different and being discriminated against has caused a lifetime of trouble for countless people across the globe, both immigrant and native-born.

It affects us everywhere, from homes, churches, and schools to the workplace and marketplace. Think of the opportunities for collaboration, friendship, and relief that are lost every day, simply because we don't understand ourselves and others who enter our world by chance and happen to belong to a country, gender, race, ethnic group, or any other group we fear.

The problem extends through every aspect of life, too. Women fear men. The elderly fear teenagers. The elite fear the poor, and the poor resent those who have more than they do. Many cisgender fear the queer and transgendered. We can see evidence of our continued failure to resolve differences in repeated serious clashes between police and Blacks, and in remaining disparities in healthcare, education, and housing.

As our world gets smaller, our accelerated exposure to one another seems to have caused us, ironically, to fall back into stances of protection. Because of fear and anxiety, we often reinforce the walls around ourselves rather than finding the courage to break them down.

No matter what a clash of cultures is based on—ethnicity, nationality, race, religion, gender, sexual preference, disability, age—it takes a toll in so many ways. How do we help those who have no idea why certain behaviors are wrong or what needs to be done? People have been working in this area for decades, but questions and fears remain.

We can't continue this way. When issues of diversity (our differences) arise and are not resolved, those issues can ruin organizations, communities, and relationships. Resolving these issues is no longer an option; it's a necessity. We must become more competent in our ability to understand, accept, and interact effectively with those who are different from us.

Shouldn't all of this increased exposure and information be making us better at diversity? Maybe. But maybe knowledge and experience are not enough. A knowledgeable person still has to be willing to understand that his or her way is not everyone's way. It's the responsibility of every human being to make a personal effort to try to bridge differences. A teacher, a pastor, a community leader sets the tone that can make or break conflicts, but it's up to each individual to be willing to first accept that people are different and then nurture a desire to connect with others from all walks of life.

Even when we are attacked and believe we are justified in self-protecting, we have to know that attacking back only makes matters worse. We have to find a way to hold back our emotions and see a confrontation from someone else as an opportunity to learn, grow, and connect. It can be painful to do. It is messy. It requires us humans to access our higher-order brain.

My research shows human beings are rarely able to change their approach to diversity unless that change is *intentional and deeply personal,* and it rarely happens without the *support and encouragement of others* who are adept in bridging the gap between differences, in part because they are *high in psychological capital and emotional intelligence.* We need individuals who have navigated this path of personal development and are willing to guide the growth of others.

What's the end game? My greatest desire is that 100 years from now, we will look back and say there was a pivotal shift in our thinking in the early part of this century that led to people learning how to authentically connect with those different from themselves. In the future, I believe we will see how this new skill of connecting resulted in an increase in synergy in organizations and communities around the United States, if not around the world—if we figure this out together. Our enhanced agility in cross-cultural situations literally could be the glue that brings together diverse elements everywhere and helps us move forward peacefully in our world.

Our next step is to understand what it will take to make this pivotal shift.

* * *

Virginia Beach was the last time I saw Agha standing up. As he walked to the plane to leave us, he turned around, waved to me and blew me one last precious kiss I will never forget.

Six months later, after suffering a heart attack and stroke upon his arrival in Detroit and then living in a "locked-in" state in the hospital, my dad, my hero, Hamzeh Ali Abdali-Soosan, died on February 19, 1992.

We were devastated—lost and shattered. Our hearts, which already had been broken so many times, were broken yet again. After much discussion, we decided to bury Agha in California, far from Iran, the home of his birth and land of his dreams, so he would be close to my mother, brother, and sister, and so he would remain in the land of his children and grandchildren.

During my dad's hospitalization, the pain and destruction of cultural *rigidity* became tangible and raw for us within the health care setting, as it has for thousands of other immigrants. I eventually would understand, as my dad laid immobile for months after his stroke, we were at our most vulnerable, both as a family and as individuals. For the capable, professional, progressive, compassionate man lying in that bed, it was the weakest, most vulnerable moment of his life. Without an ability to communicate in the language of the land, he was at the mercy of his caregivers. Our efforts to translate were only a slight buffer between his need for care and the nurse's inadequate understanding.

One moment in dad's hospital room, one comment from a nurse to her aid deriding us for not speaking English, triggered a lifetime of study and searching for me—and ultimately launched my career as a scholar, educator, and consultant in the field of diversity and inclusion. The questions began flying in my head that very day in the hospital. My father loved this country and believed the United States had the best healthcare and education in the world. But I thought to myself back then, how that can be true if we have such a high level of intolerance in health care? How do we keep from passing this level of intolerance on to those who want to work in health care?

I asked myself what role I might play in ensuring that what happened on that day with the nurse, never happens to anyone else, anywhere, whether it's in health care, education, communities, or organizations. Perhaps it's too much to ask that we could cancel out intolerance everywhere, but we have to start somewhere. I saw my personal experience with health care disparity as a call to action.

Through all the years since that day of realization in the hospital, my work in diversity has been filtered through the world of health care. Hospitals and health care settings would become my laboratory, both literally and figuratively, to study, test, and better understand what makes people fearful of others. Ultimately, I would discover that solutions revealed within health care could be migrated to any other arena of life.

I've helped students dig deep to understand and overcome their fear of each other and optimize their learning. I've helped corporate leaders formulate new approaches that settle infighting and enrich the lives of their employees, while accelerating their ability to produce more and better products and services. I've helped communities come together and connect with newcomers and embrace changing demographics in workplaces and places of worship.

All the study and experience and collaboration with others in the field of diversity led me to a conclusion that took me completely by surprise: The day the nurse insulted us in the hospital where my father lay dying, she was not the only intolerant one.

I had been *intolerant of her* in ways that were equally as damaging. I did not build a bridge that day. I chose to connect only with my own pain and close myself to any ability to understand her frustration. My response is a perfect example of when our System 2 brain goes offline. I had not felt empathy for *HER*.

Questions

1. Can you think of examples of microaggression you have experienced? Have you ever been in a situation where you have observed that someone was reacting with a joke or a statement that seemed to you out of line?
2. Can you put yourself in the shoes of that person who was at the receiving end of aggression and imagine what it would be like to experience many of these small aggressions?
3. Who has encouraged you to build a bridge between yourself and others? What did they do to help you?

6

Getting Comfortable With Change

At the first I knew not
That city's worth,
And turned in my folly
A wanderer on earth.

—A. J. Arbery

On March 16, 1992, I stood in a Norfolk, Virginia courtroom, facing a U.S. District Court judge to pledge my life and loyalty as a citizen of the United States. A representative of the Daughters of the American Revolution handed me a tiny American flag. As I looked down at that powerful symbol in my hands, I noticed the contrast between the red and white stripes and between the bright white stars and their navy background. They mimicked the contrasts of this country: rich and poor, old and young, working and unemployed, native and non-native, gay and straight, dark and light—and so many other shades of reality for so many different people.

I was excited and honored to join the United States as a legal citizen, and I felt no hesitation in the least. *This* was my destiny! I don't have photos of the moment I became a citizen of the United States, because we weren't

---

Becoming Inclusive, pages 63–78
Copyright © 2021 by Information Age Publishing
All rights of reproduction in any form reserved.

allowed to take cameras into the courtroom. But I have a rich bank of memories to mark that day. My boss, the vice president for human resources at First Hospital Corporation, Cathy Callahan, was there to witness this huge change in my life, and so was Commander George Marvin, captain of the ship where I had served as ombudsman and Scott's commanding officer. Later that afternoon when I arrived at work, my coworkers presented me with a cake decorated with a green card with a red slash through it constructed from frosting.

Citizenship meant more than you can imagine to me and my family. After everything we had gone through to keep me here, the hundreds of dollars we had spent, and the hoops we'd had to jump through to obtain my green card in 1985, this was finally the last of the steps necessary to pry me free of the "clutches" of Immigration. It was the finish line, I thought—my final destination on the road to becoming a real American.

It had been so horrible dealing with the U.S. Immigration and Naturalization Department that I still consider it to be one of the most horrific experiences I've ever had. It seemed as though leaving a dot off 1 line was justification to deny the entire application and force you to send in another one. I had never before and have never since been treated so disrespectfully by employees of a government agency—and this is the treatment I received *by INS staff*.

As I stood in the courtroom, in tears during most of the ceremony, I thought of my boys who were then not quite two and six. They were standing with my husband at the back of the chamber. I remember thinking, "They won't remember this, but more importantly they will never have to go through this." I felt a deep sense of gratitude to my husband for his devotion and willingness to see this process through to the end.

The tears rolling down my cheeks were tears of relief and happiness, but they were mingled with tears of sorrow. My father had passed away only a few weeks earlier, and I missed him. I desperately wanted to call him up and tell him about the wonderful changes about to take place in my life.

At the end of a citizenship ceremony, new Americans are given a certificate of naturalization—a piece of paper representing an exciting and longed-for new level of freedom. I eventually learned that the piece of paper doesn't have much relevance to the way people perceive or treat you. A legal citizen with a Mexican name still will be treated by some as though they just came across the border. But that day, I was beyond happy to have that certificate. The true value of citizenship is that it gives you rights. You can legally vote, for example. In some states, you have to be a citizen to buy a home, travel with a U.S. passport, stay in this country indefinitely, and more. But most importantly for me, citizenship changed the way I thought about myself.

When you come from a different country, it really takes a long time to feel like an American, even if you have become a citizen. During the time that you are "becoming an American," there's great fear and trepidation, but the citizenship papers create a sense of relief and you can relax and settle into your life. For Scott and me, this was especially momentous, because this settling-in coincided with his transition from ship duty to shore duty, and we had some exciting choices ahead of us.

One of the main reasons I became a citizen is that I wanted the power to vote. I wanted to help people and take part in the development of my new nation. Caring for others is in my nature, and I had all kinds of ideas about what I could do to help people in my new country. As a citizen of the United States, I would no longer have to look over my shoulder for the immigration department but could now face forward and find my true place in service to my fellow citizens.

*   *   *

Today, as I remember that day long ago when I received my U.S. citizenship, it is the memory of a calm moment in a raging storm. As soon as we walked away from the courtroom, our lives became filled with stressful complications, obligations, and constant pressure.

In 1993, my sister and mother returned to Iran to fulfill the Muslim ceremony and feast on the first anniversary of my father's death. Before they left the United States, we applied for green cards for both of them. Because their applications were still in process when it was time for the trip to Iran, they were required to get permission to leave the country, which they did. However, due to unforeseen complications in Iran, they missed the return deadline and the reentry permits expired.

After that, the process of getting their green cards took 5 years. During that time, my sister aged from 13 to 18 and transformed from a child into a young adult, losing her opportunity to spend one of the most important times of her life in the United States. The situation added pressure every day for us back in the states. My mom often called and asked for help, and I struggled to figure out what to do. I had become a citizen and should finally have had my peace, but I was still feeling the fear and anguish of family members who hadn't yet received that honor.

In the meantime, my dad's parents passed away in Iran. More complications! Losing a grandparent who lives in a faraway country raises many questions of logistics, honor, and emotion. How do you grieve? How do you express your pain and sorrow to the family in Iran who wants you to be there? Do you simply send flowers and notes of condolence? That isn't what my Iranian family was used to. Do you take funeral leave and travel overseas, leaving your young children and spouse behind? So many logistics. Where will we get the money for that? But how can a person mourn properly so far away from other family members—the ones who share your intimate memories of the person who has been lost?

This time was also difficult for my husband, friends, and coworkers. They were getting exposure to something they hadn't experienced before. Because I wasn't able to travel to Iran, I searched for another way to mourn. One way I dealt with my sorrow and anxiety was cooking Iranian food and inviting people over. I needed community. I needed loved ones close to me. It wasn't traditional mourning, but it was the only way I could feel as though I was doing what I needed to do. My family in Iran didn't understand. "Why can't you come to the funeral?" they asked me repeatedly. I couldn't tell them I was too poor to afford the ticket or that my kids were too young for me to leave that long. I felt constant pressure and worry.

My father's and grandparents' funerals were not the only time my family asked me to come to events overseas. When a member of my family was getting married, for example, they would ask: "Why can't you come to the wedding?" I always struggled with mixed feelings, wanting to do my duty and to see my family in Iran, but feeling powerless due to lack of funds.

After my citizenship ceremony, it was not long before it was time to leave Virginia. More complications and turmoil! It should have been an exciting time for us. Scott had had his fill of ships and wanted to be "as far away from the ocean as possible," but when he explained this to his detailer, he was told our only choices were Salt Lake City, Utah, or Lincoln, Nebraska. He was out to sea when he was offered these two duty stations, so we talked about it by phone.

Scott told me to choose between Salt Lake City and Lincoln since I hadn't seen much of the United States and had always had to move to the places the Navy sent us. I didn't know where Lincoln was, but I had heard of President Abraham Lincoln and I really liked what he had done for this country. Utah just didn't sound inviting to me. So I said, "Where is Lincoln, Nebraska?" To which Scott responded, "Open the map to the first page. See the state in the middle where the crease is? That is where Lincoln is." So we decided to check Lincoln out.

We visited the city for a house-hunting trip in August 1992, first visiting the Naval reserve station in Lincoln Airpark. As we drove toward Lincoln's downtown area, we saw Memorial Stadium rise above the downtown buildings, a magnificent and impressive sight. We walked around the University of Nebraska campus and I began to get excited about going to school again as I had promised my dad. Suddenly, the world seemed full of possibility and all of our difficulties seemed to begin receding into the past.

We moved to Lincoln, Nebraska, on November 1, 1992. This would make move number 30 for me, all before the age of 30. But we finally had found our very own place to land and put down *our own roots*. We have been in Lincoln since, and it is the place we consider home.

* * *

When I applied to the University of Nebraska–Lincoln, I was rejected.

My GPA was not good, and I can understand how it looked to the admissions officers in Nebraska. It reflected on the last semester I had attended college—my first semester at the University of South Florida. During that time, it had been difficult to study because I didn't have a place to live and was hitchhiking to school in Tampa from my friends' apartment in Clearwater.

I didn't take the rejection from UNL lightly. I called the Office of Admissions and scheduled an appointment. I explained my story to the admissions officer, explained that my circumstances had improved a great deal in the last 10 years, and said, "If you let me in, you won't regret it." It took some convincing, but they eventually relented and allowed me to enroll. I made good on my promise, and 3 years later walked in to see the admissions officer again, bachelor's degree (with distinction) in hand, and said, "I TOLD you!"

I completed my bachelor's degree in management and economics in May 1996. During that time, I was able to participate in a short summer study abroad at Oxford University in England. I studied British political economy and international economics. To finance my studies, I received several scholarships, worked part-time and completed several internships— all while raising my kids and enjoying my Nebraska life with Scott. With Scott's meager income in the military and the few part-time jobs I could fit into my schedule, we still were below the poverty line. We received benefits through the Women, Infants, and Children (WIC) program for our sons, and when they went to school, we qualified for the reduced lunch program.

While in school, I was president of a chapter of the Society of Human Resource Management. I met many people in Lincoln, and one was director of human resources at Bryan Hospital. I was impressed with the details he shared about the hospital, and it made me realize, after having worked in health care in Virginia, I wanted to use my degree to contribute to the future of health care.

When I graduated, I excitedly applied at Bryan, but the hospital didn't have any jobs at the time. I wasn't worried. They weren't going anywhere. I found a position working in human resources and accounting for a local company named Square D.

After some time at Square D, where I gained new experiences working with a unionized organization and writing an affirmative action plan, I applied to Bryan Hospital and was hired for a position as an employment coordinator, which meant recruiting employees for various divisions of the hospital. I began working at Bryan in April 1999.

In August of 1999, Bryan's director of human resources, Doug McDaniel, shared with me that he would be creating a diversity position. Through his experience with Leadership Lincoln (a community leadership development program I later would participate in), he knew diversity was growing in Lincoln and had made a personal commitment to his colleagues to increase diversity at the hospital by recruiting and retaining diverse employees.

By August 2000, I was named Bryan Health's coordinator of diversity and cultural competence. Because it was a new position, I was given limited information about what my role would entail and what my duties should be. So, I began at the beginning by conducting an organizational analysis. I met with community leaders (especially those serving diverse populations) to find out what people in their communities thought of Bryan. I asked lots of questions, listened for many hours and took lots of notes.

Do people want to work at Bryan, I asked. Is it perceived to be a good company to work for if you are a member of a diverse population group? I wanted to understand what was going on in their communities and how it affected employment for the community's members. I also met with diverse employees at Bryan Health to understand their perception of what made the organization great and what could make it better. I spoke with employees at different levels ranging from entry level to professional/management level.

Part of my recruitment duties at Bryan included conducting employee orientation, which meant I got to know people from the moment they began working at Bryan. This was very helpful in my diversity work, so I continued to facilitate new employee orientation even after my promotion. As time went on, I kept asking questions. Are you glad you work here? Do you like it? What would make this a better company for you?

As a part of my work for Bryan, I became actively involved in our city's refugee resettlement issues when I joined the New Americans Task Force (NATF). NATF was a network composed of many agencies and groups interested in helping refugees resettle in Lincoln. I became involved in that organization because I realized Bryan needed to gain an understanding of refugee health care needs, as well as provide opportunities for employment.

Gradually, I put together a picture of diversity at Bryan. To my surprise, it encompassed much more than employment and HR concerns. My interview discussions began to spill over into topics related to clinical care. Neither me nor the human resources director had expected this, but our hospital diversity program began to morph toward the clinical side.

At some point, as my diversity career blossomed during those years at Bryan, I remember thinking, "So much has happened to me in so little time." In my work as a developing professional human resources and diversity expert, I was so far removed from the frightened young girl I had been at the unfamiliar, intimidating Florida boarding school.

There is indeed hope for change in the world, I thought to myself. If I could rise to the occasion and take advantage of the opportunities that lay before me, I believed I actually might be able to play some useful role in helping create change through this very important work.

*   *   *

For years, since the incident with my dad and the nurse before his death, I had prayed I might find a way to use my experiences and my education to help bring change to health care. It was a dream come true to be put in a position at a hospital where I might have a genuine impact. I bent to the task and did everything I could to develop genuine change.

I devoured all the diversity literature and research I could. I read landmark government reports, materials from the George Washington University Center for Cultural Competence, and reports by several health care systems that had accomplished much in the area of diversity. I began poring through the information on my own time and gaining as much knowledge as I could. (I'll share some of what I learned in the coming chapters.)

During the day, I would find reports and articles, print them and bring my briefcase full of materials home at night to read and highlight. I took stacks of notes, and the more I read the more I realized Bryan's diversity initiative could not be successful without a 3-pronged approach. We had to be more effective in how we handled diversity and cultural issues with (a) our employees, (b) our patients, and (c) our community.

After I finished the organizational analysis, I met with our senior leadership team and explained my findings and recommendations. I suggested that their idea of a diversity initiative was incomplete; they envisioned simply assigning someone to do things such as putting up pictures in the hospital celebrating diverse holidays. I told them if that's what they wanted, I wasn't the person for the job and they could let me go. But if they wanted to see the hospital become more effective in meeting diverse employee and patient needs, I could help. It would mean asking difficult questions and pushing for structural change. If they were ready to do that, I explained, then I was the person for the job and I would gladly devote myself to it.

I began to look at everything as if with a microscope, attempting to learn why things worked the way they did. In general, I looked for opportunities and limitations affecting the growth of our diverse employee population. I asked many difficult questions. Why are a majority of our ethnic or racial minorities working in housekeeping and dining service? Why do we have only one senior director who is female and no person of color? From a patient care standpoint, I asked what is lacking in relation to the cultural and language needs of patients and their families. What important cultural elements of disease, diagnosis, treatment, and recovery are missing? Does our staff receive training that emphasizes a need to understand the culture of the person they are treating?

Even though Bryan had been making allowances for culture in some ways, one of our greatest gaps was a community perspective. To truly understand the needs of the culturally diverse members of a community, you have to become actively involved in the diverse community. I knew that much, and I began taking a strategic approach to diversity. There was one big obstacle in my way. I was not part of the senior leadership team, so everything I did had to go through multiple layers for approval and funding.

This made it very difficult to create momentum. A chief diversity officer (CDO) meeting with senior leaders has a different voice than a diversity coordinator whose role is to be the CDO but who is limited to focusing on only a segment of change and must follow the "chain-of-command." I was fortunate to have direct access to the hospital's senior staff and they knew very well what I was doing. But it still was difficult because I was not on their level. I had no budget to work with, so I had to be creative.

The cost of my position (my salary) already was being absorbed as part of the HR department's budget, so I didn't look there for funds. I looked for other ways to fund diversity activities. For example, I would go to patient care services with a project related to their work and say, "This is what we want to do." If they felt the project would help them reach their objectives, they would agree and fund the project. I wrote diversity content and included it in nursing orientation and new employee orientation. I went to the director of volunteer services and asked for donations to purchase wire-bound bedside books to help nurses care for diverse patients. I even went to IT services and asked if they could justify paying for online access to cultural information since the material was online.

I created a diversity council consisting of 17 employees from a variety of departments and levels in the organization. This team achieved goals that had never been thought of before. In many ways, we operated as a separate, cohesive department with a hand in multiple areas of the hospital. However, it became clear that not everyone felt diversity was as important as I did. When I pushed for resources from other departments, I sometimes felt as though I was doing something illegal, even though I had been hired to do exactly what we were doing: achieving diversity objectives.

I always felt I was operating on the edge. One day, I was in a meeting with a group of senior leaders and other employees and I said something that was not well received because I was forceful in my opinion. Later that day, a senior leader was sent to my office to talk to me about my behavior. This happened several times. I began to realize, although many in our organization were committed to diversity, this was going to be a tougher job than I had initially anticipated.

One year, a vice president position opened and a White male was hired behind closed doors. I spoke up, saying everything we had been trying to achieve was negated by that decision. I was told the person was right for the organization strategically. I admitted I didn't have access to the same information as the senior staff, but I emphasized that it didn't look good. How could an organization claim a commitment to diversity and then not open such a position to all applicants?

Eventually, being honest with everyone began to pay off. It was obvious many employees wanted to understand, even if they were having trouble with it. Some would come to my office and admit they didn't understand why a push for diversity was so important. One of them pointed out the hospital had only a 3% minority population. "Why should we care?" the person asked. I patiently explained what is routinely lost because non-majority employees tend to be dismissed and non-majority patients tend to be lumped together with the majority—and many other issues that stem from ignoring diversity.

The entire process was difficult for me personally, too. I was forcing people to think differently, behave differently, and see the world differently, and often they didn't want to. Most of them weren't ready, but I didn't understand why. I was convinced I was doing the right thing. If I had known then what it would take to sustain this effort for the long haul, I'm not sure I would have consented to do it. I already had plenty to worry about with my family, mom, and sister, and I was facing difficulties related to my own past.

* * *

When my oldest son Jonathan was in 6th grade, he began listening to rap music. I didn't get it. I didn't understand the words, many of which were cuss words. I kept thinking I didn't want him to listen to what might be bad for him. Rap didn't make sense to me—it was different from any other music I'd ever heard. One day Jonathan came home from school and said he'd been thinking about my aversion to rap music. "Everything that doesn't make sense isn't bad for you," he said.

Suddenly I understood. It explained a great deal about what was happening at work for our organizational leaders. They were uncomfortable and my work seemed ambiguous. I needed to figure out how to make it nonthreatening and reduce the ambiguity. This revelation was like a slap in the face. I had been trying to force people to trust me and it had only been making them more uncomfortable.

* * *

The Emancipation Proclamation officially set slaves free in the United States on January 1, 1863, but it would not be until 100 years later that laws were passed under the leadership of President Kennedy to finally remove barriers that kept Black citizens from voting. Our youngest son, Alan, was in fourth or fifth grade when he figured this out and asked me why it took so long. I was impressed that such a young person could ask such a perceptive question. It made me think. (We are busy raising our children, and God is using them to raise us!) It was the first time I realized change comes slowly for human beings. I believe there are many reasons we all possess this characteristic.

In their book *Spiral Dynamics,* Don Beck and Christopher Cowan (1996) explain the changes in worldview and mindset that have occurred in human history and the fact that the human brain, spirit, and soul takes hundreds of years to change. The slow pace of change in the human brain is made even slower by the complex ways the push and pull of new knowledge and technologies impacts our daily lives. We don't all understand the need for change at the same time or pace. As a result, we see the world at any given time in different ways and that can complicate our efforts to bring about change.

In some organizations, this dynamic is complicated by people in positions of power and authority who have trouble letting go of the reins. Some leaders believe that for someone to be brought up someone has to step down. When this is true, it can take generations for people to allow change to happen.

If all of this is true, I realized, it would take time to bring about change at Bryan Health—and in the world. I would have to be patient. I began to understand that I saw the world with a different mindset than most of the other leaders at the hospital. My mindset wasn't better. Theirs wasn't worse. We were just at different points in our perception of the need for change. Our differences created conflicting paces and approaches to building an inclusive organization.

I understood then that I wouldn't be able to change people's minds overnight. All of these ideas suggested that at Bryan I needed to first reach for low hanging fruit. My job was simply to do what was possible and not worry about trying to accomplish what we as a group weren't ready for.

* * *

I remember September 11, 2001, like it was yesterday. I had come into the office to prepare for a presentation I was scheduled to give that morning at the Goodwill Industries office across town. I and my coworkers huddled together in one of the hospital conference rooms to watch reports of the attack on the television. When it was time to leave for my presentation, I gathered my materials together and got ready to go. But I first called my husband to check in and get moral support. Then I called my mom, who was living in New York City at the time with my younger brother Allen, his wife, and their baby.

"Mom, is Allen okay?" I asked, thinking he had no reason to be at the Twin Towers, so the answer surely would be that he was fine.

"It's not real," my mom said to me. "It's just people saying these things. It's propaganda." Before I hung up, I asked her to please turn on the TV and watch—to see that it was indeed real—then asked her to call Allen.

At the Goodwill presentation, I didn't believe it would be a good idea for a Middle Eastern woman like me to lecture Americans on how great diversity is when the Twin Towers disaster in New York, instigated by Middle Eastern terrorists, was so raw and new. We simply used the time to talk about what had happened and how people were feeling about it.

That night, Scott and the boys and I attended a prayer vigil for the 9/11 victims at our church. (In 1993, I had converted from Muslim to Christian.) One of the things I have loved about our church is our intentional effort to create an inclusive faith community. People from all walks of life are invited and encouraged to connect with one another. After the prayer vigil, our pastor approached us and told us the local television channel was looking for a family they could interview about the way families were dealing with news of the attack. Scott and I agreed. When the television crew arrived at our home, we sat with the boys at our dining room table. The interview explored how we were talking with our kids about the tragedy.

The next day at the hospital, in one of the staff lounges, someone made a joke about that day's forecast in the Middle East. "Monday, Tuesday, and Wednesday: sunny. Thursday: nuclear cloud." They were referring to the idea that the United States could blow away any Middle Eastern target with a nuclear bomb—if it wanted to. An employee from that department who was not American born came to my office afraid and apprehensive. Did their coworkers really feel that way about it? How did they feel about us? Would any of us become the target of this hostility? I felt the same misgivings they were feeling.

Later, a Middle Eastern daycare employee at the hospital whose husband was a physician and who lived in an affluent part of town told me someone had set a bag of feces on fire, had thrown it at their front door, and had spread their garbage all over their lawn. We also heard about a Middle Eastern grocery store that was ransacked and many other incidents related to the 9/11 attack. It all reminded me of the Iranian crisis in 1979. I kept thinking to myself that things hadn't changed much since the Japanese internment camps during World War II.

On some level, within my heart, something shifted. These incidents led me to a new realization about my American citizenship: We may believe we are free and safe as immigrant citizens of the United States, but if we become a perceived threat in any way then we are still in danger. The daycare teacher and her physician husband were respected citizens of Lincoln and still they were targeted for violence by ethnocentric people.

I was relieved that my own family hadn't experienced any attacks, and then I thought it was strange. What had changed? Why were we being treated differently from others? Was it a coincidence or because people knew me in my role at the hospital? Or was it because I married a White man who had been in the military? I wanted to understand, because I believed it could help me reach out to both victims and perpetrators in these types of diversity misunderstandings.

Above all, because I was being treated well and not experiencing the violence, I became even more determined that I would not remain silent. I felt it was my duty. This realization led to a change in my attitude, an increase in my level of confidence, and a sharpening of my focus on the objectives of my work.

* * *

During a nursing shortage just after the turn of the new century, Bryan decided to recruit nurses from the Philippines because their education met U.S. government licensing requirements. They also possessed the ability to transition easily into the United States in terms of language. This was a major undertaking for Bryan, and a team was being sent to the country in the Summer of 2001 to recruit.

I hadn't been chosen for the team, but I thought I *should* be on it. I shared this with the HR director. "I can help you understand what they'll need and want to know," I explained. "I can conduct a mini orientation and prepare them and help them feel comfortable about coming to Nebraska and the hospital, then be a point of contact when they get here, and I can help them through the acculturation process." He agreed, and I became a member of the team.

In the Philippines, we interviewed more than 100 nurses and extended offers to more than 70. We expected them to arrive in Nebraska in 6 to 12 months. Because of the 9/11 attacks, their arrival was delayed and only 35 of the candidates qualified after their INS paperwork was processed. In this way, 9/11 was a setback for diversity.

We knew the nurses would be nervous about coming to the United States, so we began to put some things in place to help them adjust. Long before they arrived in Nebraska, each of the nurses was given a Nebraska pen pal, a Bryan employee who had volunteered to connect with them and begin a friendship. We recruited pen pals through the employee newsletter.

The pen pal program helped us keep in touch with the nurses and probably improved ultimate recruitment numbers because it reduced anxiety about not knowing anyone in Nebraska. The exchanges with pen pals also helped them visualize what it would be like to live here. We invited a Filipino employee to join us on the recruitment trip so he could describe his work at Bryan Hospital in their terms. As the nurses began to arrive in Nebraska, we connected them with their pen pals in person to help them feel welcome.

To assist with the recruitment effort, we created Mabuhay Guides. Mabuhay means "welcome" in Tagalog, the primary language of the Philippines. These 3-ring binders were full of important information about living in the United States and Nebraska, including material on topics ranging from housing and transportation to walking on the ice and even how to purchase a used car.

It was standard recruitment practice at Bryan to provide 90 days of housing for professional-level individuals hired from out of state. We usually placed one nurse in a house by themselves. However, knowing the collectivistic nature of the Philippines, we housed the Filipino nurses together (one nurse to each bedroom in a house) to help them avoid isolation, which we believed would have hindered their adjustment. We held celebrations for them and put them in touch with the local Filipino community.

To this day, I keep in touch through social media with many of the Filipino nurses we recruited. A few years ago, I gave a commencement speech at Southeast Community College in Lincoln, and one of the nurses' daughters was graduating from college. She had been a toddler when she arrived in the United States. It was a wonderful feeling to see that she had succeeded and to watch her family at the graduation, so proud of her as she walked across the stage and accepted her diploma.

In the months and years following that recruitment initiative, as I spoke with other organizations that had hired people from various countries, I realized how innovative our approach had been. No other organization in Nebraska at the time was onboarding international hires as comprehensively as we were. The head of international health care at the University of Nebraska Medical Center, Nizar Mamdani, inquired about our program. He was working to create a reciprocal training program for physicians through which doctors from other countries would come learn at UNMC and UNMC medical students would go to other countries to experience global health care. He and I spent several meetings discussing how we had designed these programs and the reasons behind the way they were set up.

The resettlement of refugees and immigrants, including Bryan's Filipino nurses, became a family affair at my house. We invited the nurses and other refugees and immigrants to attend community activities with us and welcomed them into our home. We even became involved with Iranian refugees in Lincoln. It was very satisfying for me, as you can imagine. It helped my sons and husband experience life with Iranians in a way they hadn't been able to with my own family members due to the geographical separation between us.

This all helped me gain confidence, and I relaxed into my role as an advocate of inclusion at the hospital and in our community. We began to make real progress at the hospital. I was seen as a valuable resource by the clinical staff and would receive calls at all hours of the day to help with issues related to diverse patients, including birth, death, and family needs. I was seen by the non-majority community as a person they could count on to help them understand American health care or seek a job.

Once I realized it would take time to address the fears of those who resisted change and transform the culture of the hospital, I decided to slow down and target my efforts toward nonthreatening activities. As a result of this change in perspective, I began focusing on what we *could do*, not what we *couldn't do*. I often asked for advice from my mentors at the hospital (two female executives), who were excited about the diversity effort and wanted to help me succeed. I figured out who had a financial stake in what we wanted to do, and then I approached those budget gatekeepers for funding.

I knew it was too early to achieve policy changes, but I could focus on small issues leading to bigger changes step-by-step. One day I heard a nurse supervisor say she wished her staff had a bedside card they could use to point to translations of common phrases such as, "Do you have your dentures?"; "Do you need your glasses?"; and "Are you thirsty?" That was the seed that grew into a spiral-bound bedside book. It was a small thing we could begin working on immediately, along with other small steps, such as ensuring minority populations knew when job positions were open. I truly felt there was hope for change in health care in our community. In fact, I believed there was hope for change in many other facets of life in all of its diversity—and I was proud to be a part of it.

I began to see that the contrasts between diverse people, like the contrasting stripes of the little flag I received on citizenship day from the Daughters of the Revolution, are a beautiful thing representing rich opportunity and do not need to be a cause for pain. The memories of pain I felt during the process of becoming American will never go away, but those bad memories began to fade as I learned positive ways to reach out and do what I could do to make a difference.

Questions

1. Who benefits when we welcome refugees and immigrants into our community?
2. Describe the differences in approach and time needed to create systemic changes versus surface solutions when it comes to inclusion. How can you be part of creating systemic changes in a workplace or organization you are part of?

7

Our Path to Cultural Competence

> *"Patience turns stones to rubies," they say.*
> *Yes! If you work hard and wait long, it may.*
>
> —S. M. Hafiz

In my role at Bryan Health, as I studied piles of materials, the history of diversity in the United States unfolded before me. I began to get a sense of all that U.S. citizens had gone through to get where we were at the time of 9/11. Understanding this background and the progression of ideas and efforts to bring about change helped me create realistic, successful diversity plans at the hospital, and perhaps most importantly provided a way for me to identify what was missing, which is how I later decided on the direction of my doctoral dissertation.

For anyone who seeks to become a catalyst for changes related to diversity, whether on a small scale (as in a church, school, or corporation) or on a grand scale (within industries, regions, and the world), an understanding of the progress we've made thus far is critical. Without this understanding, we are liable to make the same mistakes, become confused, go over the same ground, misdirect our efforts, and lose what we've gained as a society.

Becoming Inclusive, pages 79–95
Copyright © 2021 by Information Age Publishing
All rights of reproduction in any form reserved.

I encourage readers to patiently consume the following information and think about how and why some of these developments came about. Allow the knowledge to rest in your mind and provide context for the changes you are hoping to make in your own microcosm of diversity.

You also may be able to pull information from this chapter to help lead others to understand these unfolding diversity-related events as they grapple with the concept and seek ways to make changes. It is my hope that the knowledge you gain here helps you feel as hopeful and excited about change as it did me in my evolving role at Bryan. Knowledge always leads to possibilities.

*   *   *

The horror of the Tuskegee syphilis experiment became common knowledge in 1973 and could not help but shed light on health care disparity among Blacks. The U.S. government couldn't *not* act! As people became aware of what had been happening, I can imagine the many conversations and meetings that must have taken place to try to figure out what to do about it. The eye-opening revelation about the Tuskegee study led to formation of a task force in 1980, which resulted in creation of the Office of Minority Health (OMH) and an official study of the issues related to racial disparity in health care.

The task force, sponsored by the Department of Health and Human Services (DHHS), in 1985, released its "Report of the Secretary's Task Force on Black and Minority Health," also known as the Heckler report. It was named after Margaret Heckler, the United States' 15th secretary of health and human services. The task force had conducted research in what became known as "a landmark effort in analyzing and synthesizing the present state of knowledge of the major factors that contribute to the health status of Blacks, Hispanics, Asians/Pacific Islanders, and Native Americans." It was the first time DHHS had put minority health issues into a single report.

In the cover letter accompanying the report, Heckler very forcefully emphasized the history of disparity leading to death and illness for Blacks and other minority Americans, revealing that the disparity had existed ever since the beginning of accurate federal recordkeeping. She recognized the fact that steady gains were being made in the health status of minority Americans, but she confirmed that "the stubborn disparity remained—an affront both to our ideals and to the ongoing genius of American medicine."

The 264-page report identified eight recommendations ranging from education of the population and health care providers to increased funding and research. At last, the United States government was recognizing the problem officially. Maybe this was the beginning of the end of ignoring the issue. At the very least, it opened the door to more discussion and more connection between people who could analyze what had been happening, so they could help the nation move toward positive, meaningful solutions. The Heckler report called for more research. Although by that time we understood much more about *what* was happening, we still didn't really understand *why* it was happening or *what to do about it.*

In 1986, just a year after the Heckler report was released, Congress created the Office of Minority Health (OMH) by congressional mandate. The OMH Resource Center was formed as a one-stop source for minority health literature, research, and referrals for consumers, community organizations, and health professionals. The center offered information and resources related to health issues specifically pertaining to African Americans, American Indians and Alaska Natives, Asian Americans, Hispanics, Native Hawaiians, and Pacific Islanders.

Making information and resources available about the special health care needs of minorities was a necessary first step to helping all stakeholders understand and deal with what had been happening—it was a foundation upon which Americans could continue to build a new framework for inclusive health care. Patients back then, much like the Afghani woman and her family a couple of decades later, desperately needed solutions to trickle down to the level of individual care. But it would take some time. It would take another decade and a half for the nation to analyze the facts, work together to understand them, and then formally outline steps that should be taken to change our health care system for the better.

In 1998, after years of research and providing health care information for minorities, OMH sponsored a study in conjunction with the Agency for Healthcare Research and Quality (AHRQ) to formally determine whether health care disparities truly existed for minorities and, if they did, how they affected the delivery and outcomes of care. Through this study, the groundwork was laid to collect and analyze data and make new recommendations, and the findings created a heightened understanding of the underlying causes of disparity.

Figure 6.1 visually presents the study's findings, which were released in 2003. It was the first time any study specifically defined the nature of the disparity between nonminority and minority patients. The study, titled "Unequal Treatment: Confronting Racial and Ethnic Disparities in Health Care," was conducted on behalf of OMH and AHRQ by the Institute of Medicine (IOM).

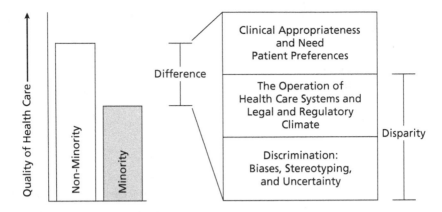

Figure 6.1 Visual of findings of IOM study (IOM, 2003, p. 3).

The three sections of the chart encompassed within the "difference" range identify ways the study found that health care quality was lacking for minorities. The first section ("Clinical Appropriateness and Need" & "Patient Preference") represents differences within the patients themselves, which were not seen as issues that could be addressed by outside forces. The second two sections are, however, areas that could be addressed, and thus those sections (marked "Disparity") define what was then seen as the gap in quality care: regulation/operations and discrimination.

The recommendations of the disparity study were more than simply a decree to examine, understand, and modify requirements. They were, in effect, a call to transform the old health care delivery system into a brand-new type of (inclusive) health care delivery system that had not existed before. Some would argue such a fundamental transformation would be impossible. Others would argue it would be difficult, yes, but not impossible. It was too important to be impossible.

The conclusion of the IOM (2003) study was clear: "The committee finds strong evidence for the role of bias, stereotyping, prejudice, and clinical uncertainty from a range of sources, including studies of social cognition and 'implicit' stereotyping, and urges more research to identify how and when these processes occur" (p. 178). The research recommendations of the IOM focused on three broad levels:

1. health care systems changes, specifically legal and regulatory changes;
2. health care worker cultural competence to address implicit prejudices, stereotyping, and bias; and

3. patient-centered care that seeks to understand appropriateness from the patient's perspective.

One of the greatest accomplishments of the OMH study is that it named the problems: bias, discrimination, and stereotyping at the individual, institutional, and health system levels. Once the problems had names, it was easier to talk about, visualize, recognize, and begin solving them. In addition to naming the problems, the study provided explicit recommendations to eliminate health care disparities. At that point, patients, families, doctors, and others who cared about the negative experiences of minorities in health care could expect that specific actions soon would be taken to improve patient care.

When results of the OMH study were published in 2003, health care disparity among minorities reached the ears of enough people that it became a tipping point. It was then that the right people came together and said, "We need to get Congress to do something about this."

And so, discovery of the gross injustice at Tuskegee was one stepping-stone to change, the Heckler report was another, creation of the OMH was another, and the government study of disparity still another. It is clear to me that these four steps among innumerable related conversations, questions, examinations of the facts, and behind-the-scenes efforts that must have taken place on the part of many, many intelligent, motivated, caring individuals led to the call for change. It was a winding path of development that you won't be surprised to know is, as far as I can see, still unfolding in the same winding, imprecise manner, but that's really okay. It's the only way we humans seem to be able to get things done.

The three broad initiatives described in this chapter have affected many aspects of health care over time, from adjustments in government agency reimbursement requirements and modification of standards of quality care for culturally and linguistically diverse populations to changes in the way quality care is assessed and training requirements are upgraded for accredited medical and health care schools.

The real test, however, would be in local hospitals and other medical institutions. Would individual caregivers' behavior really change? Would administrators and leaders know how to assess the care of unique individual minority patients in their institutions and define the problems? Would they meet resistance to change, and how would they go about planning for change? Would medical care for non-majority populations really be transformed, or would we as a nation find ourselves stuck in a holding pattern?

*   *   *

When the Afghani woman entered Bryan hospital with her daughter and son-in-law for treatment, she entered a health care system that was not ready for her—even though those who were caring for her without a doubt cared *about* her. In all medical institutions, as with the Tuskegee study, our ignorance of people unlike ourselves blinds us to what is fair and right, in spite of our best intentions.

While many health care workers are deeply empathetic to the needs of their patients, there are those who have grown calloused. This can be attributed to many factors. When my father was dying, we needed compassion badly as a family, but the nurse could only focus on the fact that we were speaking a different language, incorrectly assuming my dad didn't want to learn to speak English. I assume she could only be angry with us because she didn't understand, and then I became angry with her, perpetuating the distance between us. This is an example of how disparities can deeply affect patient care.

If we dig a little deeper, we see disparity affecting health care in ways other than individual care. Think about the way health care is paid for. If you are living on a low socioeconomic level and have little education, you likely have greater health care needs because you don't have some of the advantages affluent people often have to help them maintain their health. Chances are you have put off getting help to address your health care needs, and therefore by the time you decide to get medical care your minor needs may have become long-term needs. If you distrust medical services in the community where you live, you might wait until the last minute to seek care or end up in the emergency room, which is costlier. Many low-income people of all cultures suffer from drug addiction and alcoholism, which means they will have yet another need for long-term care they probably can't afford. And they likely don't have insurance to help them pay for it.

If you are well-to-do, you can go to the doctor any time you need to and get things taken care of before they become serious problems, so your health care costs are lower, you need care less often, and you have more money to pay for it, not just because you make more money but because your ability to promptly care for yourself leads to fewer dollars needed for care overall. If you need a kidney, you can afford insurance, so it will be paid for and your out-of-pocket costs will be much lower than those of a patient who does not have insurance or doesn't have insurance as good as yours.

This demonstrates a disparity in the way health care is funded—and solutions are not where the problems are. The point is that health care disparity isn't just about the way people are treated when they are misunderstood. It goes much deeper than that. Disparity runs through the very body of health care, as systemic diseases run through the veins and arteries of human bodies. The U.S. health care system in particular is extremely complex. And so the answers will be complex. This is likely to be true of disparity no matter what arena of life it appears in—not just health care.

Because it's difficult to understand the complexity of health care disparity, we tend only to address it on the surface. We put a bandage on the problem and believe it will change everything. For example, we believe immigrants should learn English when they decide to come to this country. So, our solution to a language problem is to get interpreters, when we really should be asking ourselves what hurdles at all cultural levels must patients get over before they even can think about learning another language. A drunk person might be put into detox for 24 hours, then released and told to go to outpatient therapy, but there may be a much deeper need for intense long-term care to modify how such patients see themselves in what they are perceiving as a hostile environment. Until those issues are addressed in a way patients themselves can understand, as well as addressing interrelated issues even they themselves may not understand, the surface solutions are likely to fail in the end or only barely provide relief.

It's not possible for us to explain the challenges and complexities of the health care system in this book, but it is important for us to understand in general that people are slipping through the system or never even reaching it and not receiving the care they need and deserve as much as anyone else. It's no different in health care than it is in other arenas of our world. The same problems with disparity are happening in law enforcement, education, housing, even restaurant service. Just knowing and acknowledging there is a problem that may go deeper than we have realized is the first step toward meaningful change.

*   *   *

Now, let's focus in a little closer on what might have been happening to *people* involved in health care changes not long after Tuskegee. The wheels of government and industry turn slowly, but you would have thought the shock of a situation like Tuskegee would have precipitated change immediately throughout government agencies and health care institutions nationwide. Such was not the case. It took *7 years* before the task force was formed!

What was missing? There were, no doubt, people who cared about this situation and wanted to make changes. Why was it years before substantial and meaningful transformations would happen?

Clues can be found in diversity studies conducted in the early 1990s and early 2000. The Heckler report recommendations had been an amazingly important step toward change, but the report hadn't uncovered something very important: how people could make change happen. And that was still missing even after the creation of the Office of Minority Health.

The world continued to wrestle with all of the issues of diversity as researchers and other stakeholders in health care continually built upon one another's ideas and findings. I personally remember what it was like around the turn of the new century. As each new idea was uncovered, it sparked more new ideas. It suddenly became okay to be a "believer" in cultural equality, identify the problems, and dig for solutions—even to embrace this process and make it a part of our personal lives and goals.

Then new findings emerged that helped us understand more.

- Transformation of a large system (such as the health care delivery system, a health care community, or a hospital) first requires transformation of multiple organizations and smaller systems (Bass & Avolio, 1994).
- Individual transformation will be necessary to bring forth organizational transformation (Bass & Riggio, 2005).
- Individual transformation in worldview is typically a product of growth and development (Hammer et al., 2003).
- As individuals grow in their understanding of the complexity of human behavior and how culture influences beliefs, attitudes, and biases, they are able to develop in intercultural sensitivity (Bennett, 1993).
- Development requires intentionally taking a deep dive and evaluating one's beliefs, values, biases, stereotypes, and assumptions held as truths on multiple levels: macrocultural level (national and/or regional), microcultural level (organization or educational institution), and individual level (familial). This developmental work takes time, can be painful, and involves a willingness to accept ambiguity with the ever-changing patient population (Gardenswartz et al., 2010).
- Historically, much of the education and training of health care providers' cultural competence has focused on having cultural knowledge and gaining cultural encounters with a variety of cul-

tures that the provider may encounter (Campinha-Bacote, 2002; Leininger & MacFarland, 2002; Papadopoulos, 2003).

▪ Even though the IOM researchers stated that the existence of disparities in health outcome is partially due to provider discrimination, bias, stereotyping, and uncertainty, there have been few empirical studies that have identified a process for development (Altshuler et al., 2003; Huckabee & Matkin, 2012); explicitly, that assertion refers to studies that are seeking to answer how the developmental level of intercultural sensitivity of health care educators affect the development of future health care providers in a measurable way. This has created a gap in effectively preparing health care providers to care for patients in the 21st century.

▪ To become culturally competent, or culturally agile, health care providers need to be educated in environments that have created a climate of respect for diversity, where unique faculty, staff, and student qualities and differences are viewed as assets to be integrated as enhancements to the organizational effectiveness, rather than issues to be detached so people can be assimilated into the organization (Douglas et al., 2011).

▪ Future health care workers are not able to develop this level of cultural competence unless they are taught and led through the process in colleges, by faculty and staff who are developmentally able to teach and engage students in a process of growth and development that is transformational in nature (Campinha-Bacote, 2002; Long, 2012).

Taken together, these findings describe the piece that had been missing: personal development toward cultural competence. The findings also indicate that this kind of personal development depends upon education in a culturally diverse environment, with leadership by culturally competent mentors and leaders.

In 2013, OMH officially named cultural competency as one of the key attributes needed to close the disparities gap in health care. According to their website, "Cultural competency is the way patients and doctors can come together and talk about health concerns without cultural differences hindering the conversation but enhancing it. Quite simply, health care services that are respectful of and responsive to the health beliefs, practices and cultural and linguistic needs of diverse patients can help bring about positive health outcomes" (https://minorityhealth.hhs.gov/omh/browse.aspx?lvl=2&lvlid=53, para. 2).

The Afghani woman and her family at Bryan are a great example. Knowing what was important to them as defined by their unique multi-layered culture, and having the cultural competency to allow them to be themselves throughout the process of providing care, not only helped avoid misunderstandings and disparities but went much farther, to creating a positive health care environment where she would have the best possible chance to thrive.

Going further than simple health care outcomes, OMH identifies other specific ways culture and language can directly influence health care (OMH, n.d.):

- health, healing, and wellness belief systems;
- how illness, disease, and their causes are perceived, both by the patient/consumer and health care providers;
- behaviors of patients/consumers who are seeking health care and their attitudes toward health care providers; and
- delivery of services by providers who look at the world through a limited set of values, which can compromise access for patients from other cultures.

To achieve equal access to quality health care, the OMH website says, the provider and the patient must transcend the individual learned patterns of language and culture they bring to the health care experience.

* * *

As all of this was going on at a high level in government, social science, and the national hallways of medicine, I was working in smaller arenas in the health care industry. I first worked in human resources at a hospital in Virginia, where I spoke constantly with my coworkers about what had happened to my dad and our family. I encouraged anyone I came into contact with, everywhere I went, to become aware of the way individuals were being treated. The seed of an idea kept growing in my mind: what if we could create a tangible process by which people could honestly transform their assumptions about those who are different from them? What would that process look like? Would leaders in medical institutions allow this process and transformation to happen or, better yet, would they be willing to champion it? Diversity was not the main focus of my job at that time, but it most definitely was never far from my thoughts.

In Virginia, I had found my place after many years of struggle. I had found my happiness with Scott and the boys, and I had a wonderful job where I was allowed to help people every day (my personal calling). My human resources work at the hospital and my position as a one-time immigrant working as ombudsman on Scott's ship were perfect places for me to begin watching these amazing developments in diversity unfold.

*   *   *

In 2001, I began to deeply understand the impact of the developmental mindset and its relationship to cultural competence, diversity, and inclusion when I completed an assessment of myself that rocked me to the core. The assessment stated that I was in a stage of cultural competence called "minimization." How could that be, I thought? There has to be something wrong with the assessment. I couldn't possibly be ONLY in minimization. I was shocked! I was sure if others found out, I'd be fired.

But how was it possible? I had created a diversity program and was leading it. I had lived in three countries and five different states in the United States. I possessed bilingual fluency in Farsi and English, with some knowledge of Latin, French, and Spanish. I had traveled to more than 20 nations and 43 states in the United States. I had helped people from numerous walks of life in my role at Bryan Health. I was active with immigrants and refugees, as well as international student populations in our community. Yet, I was in minimization.

I decided the assessment was broken. Or I had broken the assessment. That was it. It seemed to me a logical explanation, until I studied the theoretical concepts behind it all: the developmental model of intercultural sensitivity (DMIS). And then I unpacked my own experiences using the DMIS: the nurse's actions when my father was dying, my actions when I verbally attacked the nurse, the decisions made by parents and health care administrators when a Native American family allowed the organs of their 12-year-old son to be harvested for the first time in Nebraska history.

It became obvious to me that *having cultural experiences* is not the same as *having a developmental mindset* that leads to cultural competence. I began exploring why this is true. In my reading, I discovered that minimization looks different for those who are of the non-dominant (minority) in society. We minimize our differences (assimilate) as a way to get along with the majority (those in power). That is probably what I had been doing.

This was a very important revelation for me. Remember how I didn't admit to being Iranian for many years? I made sure our sons had American-sounding names, so they wouldn't be treated the way my brothers and I had been treated during our first years in this country. I noted, with deep anguish, that I had never taught my children Farsi. I hadn't wanted them to be picked on because they sounded strange. In these ways, I had unconsciously lived in minimization as a "go along to get along strategy."

As I began reading research related to developmental levels and intercultural sensitivity, I began to understand why it's not enough to study abroad or learn another language or teach people what to do with patients of various cultures (as we were prone to do in health care). The more I learned, the more I felt compelled to change myself—and not only to grow personally but to conduct research that would help others grow.

*   *   *

In 1993, 8 years after the Heckler report and 5 years before OMH began its study on health care disparities, Dr. Milton Bennett published an explanation of how individuals shift in intercultural sensitivity. He explained that intercultural sensitivity increases as individuals manage interactions with diverse others and are sensitized to differences. When you interact with people who are different from you, *noticing* the differences between your cultural beliefs and behaviors and theirs is the start of a shift in intercultural sensitivity within yourself. That ability to notice differences comes from an awareness that you have been socialized to believe, behave, and think in a way that is different—not better, not worse, just different—than others.

Becoming aware of differences is what leads a person to become interested in developing intercultural sensitivity, and that increased interest results in a shift from an *ethnocentric* mindset to an *ethnorelative* mindset. As research progressed in the years after Dr. Bennett's findings, the language describing these mindsets has changed from ethnocentric to *monocultural* and from ethnorelative to *intercultural*. A person's pausing to intentionally make this shift is a function of our slow, System 2 brain. By contrast, as I explained earlier in this book, in situations where our emotions are triggered and the fast-moving, instinctual System 1 brain takes over, it's hard for us to remain objective and suspend judgement long enough to make changes.

In addition to defining this mindset shift within people, Bennett said intercultural sensitivity involves reaching a basic understanding that cultures vary profoundly in the way they shape worldviews. This might seem obvious, but Bennett believed people don't always realize other cultures are fundamentally different from their own. Before we can develop a true shift in mindset, we have to face this fact and understand how those differences profoundly affect human perceptions and interactions.

Bennett's research shifted my perspective of what would need to happen for diversity efforts to be successful. It also provided a seed of awareness that led me to the subject of my own research (more about that later).

The six stages of Dr. Bennett's developmental model of intercultural sensitivity (DMIS) were introduced to the world in 1986 (See Figure 6.2). The model was based on Bennett's observations and interactions with many individuals as they learned to become more competent communicators in environments involving multiple cultures. The model identifies culture as any group with a set of similar constructs. Therefore, the intent of the model is not limited to racial, cultural, and ethnic diversity. Rather, all forms of diversity and differences among individuals may be included in this definition.

The DMIS represents a scale in which each of the six stages is characterized by increasing sensitivity to cultural difference. The stages assume that, as intercultural challenges cause a person's experiences of cultural difference to become more complex, the person's awareness of differences during intercultural encounters increases. It follows that this increased awareness in turn gives us the ability to better navigate such encounters.

Through testing, using the same assessment tool that judged me to be in minimization, we can see a person move up or down the scale. The assessment is called the intercultural development inventory (IDI). As a person's experience with cultural difference becomes more complex and their competence in intercultural relationships is strengthened, the person's placement on the scale moves up.

The first three DMIS stages are ethnocentric (i.e., one's own culture is experienced as central to the understanding of others). The second three stages are ethnorelative (i.e., one's own culture is experienced within the context of other cultures). Figure 6.2 is a graphic representation of the stages, followed by a description of each stage (Bennett, 1993).

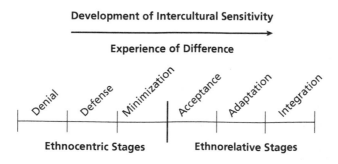

Figure 6.2   Development of intercultural sensitivity.

The Six Stages of DMIS (Bennett, 2017)

1. *Denial:* "The default condition of DMIS is the denial of cultural difference—the failure to perceive the existence or the relevance of culturally different others. Perceptual categories for otherness are not elaborate enough to allow discriminations among different kinds of others, who may be perceived vaguely as 'foreigners' or 'minorities' or not perceived at all."

2. *Defense:* "When the resolution of Denial issues allows it, people can move into the experience of defense against cultural difference. The perceptual structure of this stage is a dichotomous categorization of 'us and them,' where others are perceived more fully than in Denial but also in highly stereotyped ways."

3. *Minimization:* "The resolution of 'us and them' allows the move to the minimization of cultural difference. As the term implies, cultural differences that were initially defined in Defense are now minimized in favor of the assumedly more important similarities between self and others. However, Minimization obscures deep cultural differences."

4. *Acceptance:* "Movement out of the ethnocentric condition of Minimization allows cultural difference to be organized into categories that are potentially as complex as one's own. In other words, people become conscious of themselves and others in cultural contexts that are equal in complexity but different in form. The acceptance of cultural difference does not mean agreement..."

5. *Adaptation:* "Resolving the issue of ethicality allows the move to adaptation to cultural difference. The perceptual mechanism is that of 'perspective taking' or empathy. This is a kind of context-shifting, assumedly enabled by a neurological executive function, that allows one to experience the world 'as if' one was participating in a different culture."

6. *Integration:* "The resolution of authentic identity allows for the sustainable integration of cultural difference into communication. On a personal level, Integration is experienced as a kind of developmental liminality, where one's experience of self is expanded to include the movement in and out of different cultural worldviews."

There is no doubt the DMIS is seminal to our understanding of development and growth in intercultural sensitivity at this time in history. And the IDI assessment, developed by Bennett's colleague Mitch Hammer was published in 2003 (Hammer et al., 2003), expands the DMIS by creating a valid and reliable assessment for measuring developmental levels. However, as Bennett says, "It does not assume that progression through the stages is

1-way or permanent" (Bennett, 1993, p. 7). His writings indicate that it's possible to build up personal "patterns or categories" of perception that help us better organize our understanding and more effectively deal with issues of diversity:

> The most basic theoretical concept in the DMIS is that experience (including cross-cultural experience) is constructed. This is the central tenet of cognitive constructivism, which holds that we do not perceive events directly. Rather, our experience of events is built up through patterns or categories that we use to organize our perception of phenomena. (Bennett, 2004, pp. 72–73)

This means, as Bennett explains, that we assign *different* meanings to our experiences with diversity depending on the specific developmental level we are in at a given time (Bennett, 1993).

With this new deep understanding of human behavior in the face of diversity, the world was ready not only to admit there were biases in health care, as the OMH study found, but to begin envisioning what we could do about it to make sure nothing like Tuskegee ever happens again.

*   *   *

The OMH study was evidence of the pressure the government was feeling to come up with mandates related to health care disparity, and it became the driving force for change in countless hospitals, doctor's offices, welfare offices, and other settings where those in any minority cultural group were at risk for mistreatment in the health care system—even non-majority cultural groups unrelated to race and nationality, such as those defined by gender or age.

Our hospital already had been taking some of the actions the OMH study recommended. We considered the study to be much-appreciated, inspiring, and energizing confirmation that we had done the right thing when we decided to go out on a limb and make diversity initiatives a mandate in our small community. What I wanted to do, other people were doing all over the country. My friends joked that I was ahead of my time, which is ironic because I'd always thought of myself as a late bloomer due to my slow process of acculturation. In this one thing, perhaps because of the long and difficult road I had traveled, I understood more about the issues than most.

I recommended a three-pronged approach for our diversity and cultural competence initiative at the hospital. All activities under each prong connected with the hospital's overall strategic goals:

1. Create an inclusive organization where employees feel they are accepted and respected and have opportunities to learn and grow.
2. Become the kind of health care organization where patients feel they are heard, cultural differences are understood, and people are cared for in an environment that helps them heal.
3. Become the kind of organization that understands the needs of the changing community and engages with the community in such a way that it can meet diverse needs.

In 2006, a third influential study conducted by The Joint Commission laid out a roadmap that even more narrowly defined actions needed to create changes in the medical care of minorities. By coincidence, I heard about this study when researchers were looking for institutional participants. At a conference in Washington, DC, I happened to meet the study's chief investigator. She contacted me later and invited our hospital to participate.

The Joint Commission researchers came to our facility to interview our CEO, me in my role as the person leading the diversity and cultural competence initiatives at our health system, and other nonclinical staff, as well as clinical caregivers. It gave me a fascinating glimpse into the way research works, and the processes of that research team ultimately would provide inspiration and ideas for some of my later work and diversity research.

I have to say that it was a heady time for me. I began to see hope everywhere I looked, both personally and professionally. There was still a great deal to do in the area of health care disparity, but the changes had only begun several decades before, which to me meant there still was time and opportunity for *everyone* to learn and grow.

I still felt an inordinate amount of personal stress lingering after all the difficult experiences I had endured as a member of a "hated" minority. But people were openly discussing these health care issues and grappling with them every day instead of simply ignoring them, and I was extremely excited to be a part of it.

I felt as though I was right where I belonged: in a front row seat within the theater of diversity, where we all truly had the power to create real change, and with a sincere personal hope that I'd have what it would take to see this fiery cause through to some definable happy ending, at least in our hospital and our community.

Questions

1. How are the health care issues in this chapter similar to diversity issues in your own life?
2. Do you remember a time when you experienced problems with a health care provider? Who did you expect to take responsibility for the problem—the institution or a person?
3. It took the government many years to stop looking at the problem and start looking at solutions. Are you ready to start looking at solutions for the diversity issues in your life, or do you need some time to increase your level of cultural competency first, so you first can truly understand the problems?

8

Courage and Humility

If you lose your head but gain a kingdom,
It's a silly bargain, far from wisdom.

—S. M. Hafiz

During my time leading the diversity and cultural competence work at Bryan Health, the organization evaluated the expansion of women and baby units, in part by conducting focus groups with women. Results showed there was a need for expansion of these services because the community was growing and changing. I met with the VP leading the initiatives and asked if anyone had thought to conduct focus groups with the rapidly growing immigrant and refugee populations in our community. She was surprised by my question but was humble enough to say no and courageous enough to give me the green light and funding to conduct the focus groups with a goal of creating inclusive women's and children's health services.

I conducted focus groups with Hispanic, Middle Eastern, Asian, and African women, then presented the results of our research to the leadership team in a report titled, "Understanding the Health Care Challenges and Needs of Immigrant and Refugee Women in Lincoln, Nebraska." The

Becoming Inclusive, pages 97–110
Copyright © 2021 by Information Age Publishing
All rights of reproduction in any form reserved.

research influenced the design, layout, structure, and process of health care delivery of the new Women's and Children's Health Services wing at Bryan Health. The head of the division was hired specifically with the needs our study had identified in mind.

Because our VP had the courage and humility to allow this fundamental change at Bryan, we were able to make genuine strides forward in the ability of our hospital to address the needs of our diverse patients.

The more I have worked in the area of diversity, inclusion, and cultural competence, the clearer it has become that developing an inclusive mindset takes a certain level of willingness on the part of any individual—and that this is a lifelong endeavor requiring a great deal of effort and courage, in part because the effort is more complex than most people would believe. The reality is that this kind of personal change is necessary if the world as a whole is to become more inclusive. There are challenges only those with an inclusive mindset can resolve.

And there's no time to waste. An inability to deal with the complexity of differences among us is causing societal problems in every nook and cranny of our world. Every day, we see racially motivated violence on television, hear about modern-day genocide, even overhear people in public places disparaging others because of race, ethnicity, religion, nationality, socioeconomic status, sexual orientation, or other differences. It is apparent that we have a long way to go—and we need to get there as soon as we can. We cannot afford to further lose touch with each other and become more divisive. The greater the diversity (differences between us), the higher the likelihood there will be serious challenges facing us in the decades to come, unless we intentionally grow into a collective inclusive mindset.

I do not consider myself an expert. I am still a work in progress on both a personal and professional level. As my mother has told me on multiple occasions, "As long as you're breathing, you must be open to learning." I'm constantly gaining new insights and realizing new ways of seeing the world. It is challenging work, but I have to do it anyway, because it's important to me.

The more frequent and more involved our connection with diverse peoples of the world, the greater the complexity of differences we must learn to navigate. Learning how to navigate these differences effectively and positively is not easy. It takes intentional effort. Our ability to more effectively navigate differences doesn't just happen.

For example, when a client is speaking to us in a computer call, the computer can translate foreign words instantly, so we don't give a thought to the fact that the client is speaking from the context of a completely different culture. Learning to navigate differences well demands greater cultural self and other awareness, as well as deeper and more frequent connection with others who look, think, and believe differently than we do. Even when we do have an opportunity to connect more, we unfortunately don't always handle those interactions well.

I believe it is not overdramatic to say our very survival as a species depends on our ability to connect with each other in an empathetic embrace because of our differences—an ability many don't quite yet possess. Cultivating that ability will take humility, courage, and patience on an individual level first. The birthplace of humility, courage, and patience is authentically connecting with oneself and one's own experiences.

A high level of authenticity is required to truly connect with those who are different from us, and to gain that authenticity we must have the courage to dig deep and connect with the values, beliefs, and attitudes tied to the past events, people, and places that have shaped us. Most of us would rather not do that level of digging. We would rather not "cry over spilled milk." We'd rather "pull ourselves up by our bootstraps" than have to be still, in the solitude needed to connect, unpack, understand, embrace, grieve, and make sense of who we are and the crucible moments that have shaped us.

In this context, when I think about my reaction to the nurse all those years ago when my dad was ill, I realize I spoke my mind without thinking. My response was the result of unresolved emotions from my early years in this country when I felt forced to assimilate rather than encouraged to acculturate.

Because sick or injured patients and their families are so vulnerable, and because humans have to visit a doctor or go to a hospital at some point in our lives, a hospital or doctor's office is a perfect place to examine, understand, and solve issues related to diversity, inclusion, and the role of cultural competence in all of it. Health care has been the door through which I have been able to step to help me understand my personal issues, find a purpose for my life, and discover a way to serve. Eventually, I was able to apply the lessons I learned in health care about diversity, inclusion, and cultural competence to other venues: education, religion, business, and community. But health care is where the questions and clarifications began for me.

If you are not a member of the health care community, you may think the ideas presented in the rest of the chapter are not applicable to your own work. Maybe you are pastor of a church, teacher of a class, leader in a community, or CEO of a corporation. Maybe you are simply a thoughtful friend who wants to speak authentically about discrimination or a parent who wants to prepare your children for successfully navigating life in this global environment. I encourage you to read the chapter with your own situation in mind. These lessons of inclusion and cultural competence apply to nearly any situation. If you read between the lines, you will gain a greater understanding of how diversity challenges us within any area of life and you'll find ideas to apply in your own world.

* * *

The World Health Organization (WHO) has identified nurses as the largest group of health care professionals in the world. However, there's still a shortage of nurses and it's expected to worsen, weakening health care systems and blocking achievement of global health care goals. It is commonly believed that shortfalls in the teaching, training, development, and compensation of health care workers adds to this shortfall by discouraging pursuit of health care jobs and reducing the effectiveness of health care workers.

At the Third Global Forum for Human Resources for health care, Doctor Carissa Etienne, WHO regional director for the America, stated:

> One of the challenges for achieving extensive health coverage is ensuring access to well-trained, culturally sensitive and competent health care staff. The best strategy for achieving this is by guaranteeing that the education and training of health professionals is aligned with the needs of the population. (WHO, 2013).

According to the U.S. Census Bureau, the world's population in the future will be considerably older and more racially and ethnically diverse. As the U.S. population continues to grow in diversity—including but not limited to cultural and ethnic diversity—it will be increasingly important to align the training of health care workers with the needs of the population and improve the cultural agility of caregivers.

We seem to have a decent start with the increased awareness of health care disparities that came after the report on the Tuskegee study. Since then, many professionals with ties to health care began to examine this phenomenon, and our collective understanding of the issues deepened.

Since the IOM's landmark 2003 publication identified the three specific reasons for widespread health care disparities (bias, discrimination, and stereotyping at the individual, institutional, and health system levels), there has been an increased focus in multiple agencies on reducing health care disparities. Some of the agencies working on this include the American

Hospital Association (AHA), Centers for Medicare and Medicaid Services (CMS), the Joint Commission and Agency for Healthcare Research and Quality (AHRQ), Office of Minority Health (OMH), and the American Academy of Colleges of Nurses (AACN; Starr et al., 2011).

The idea of individuals becoming culturally competent or culturally agile isn't new to health care. Dr. Madeleine Leininger, a nurse anthropologist, was thought to be the pioneer in providing culturally meaningful care through the training of her nurses. Her work in "transcultural nursing" began in the 1950s and is widely used in nursing education and by other fields of health care (Allen, 2010).

Transcultural nursing is defined as "concerned with comparing differences and similarities between cultures regarding caring values and life practices to predict care needs of individuals and promote culturally fitting care" (Allen, 2010, p. 315).

Transcultural nursing defines culture as "attitudes, values, beliefs and life practices learned and shared by people in a particular social group which are passed on down through generations affecting individuals' thinking and actions" (Allen, 2010, p. 315).

Leininger emphasized culture-specific care, which refers to nurses' understanding of what constitutes caring actions based on available health care information and knowledge. Culture-specific care includes folk healing practices particular to each culture to provide care matching an individual's health care needs—and their expectations. Transcultural nursing's call to organizations and schools was to develop "cultural competence" as a core competence for all current and future health care providers (Betancourt, 2003; Douglas et al., 2011; Giger et al., 2007; IOM, 2003).

Businesses heavily use cultural intelligence (CQ) as a model for cultural competence, and health care institutions rely on models of cultural competence that stem from transcultural nursing. The three models most often cited in health care research are: Campinha-Bacote's model of cultural competence process (2002), Giger and Davidhizar's transcultural assessment model (2002), and Purnell's transcultural assessment model (2002).

The three models have this in common: They focus on cultural competence defined as meaningful and helpful care for people from different cultural backgrounds, founded in knowledge of specific cultural beliefs, attitudes, and practices. Each model identifies a different way to approach the assessment and development of culturally competent health care workers, and each model also contains some clues to training culturally competent people in other avenues of life.

* * *

July 25, 2007, began like most other days, except for one thing. I wasn't feeling well. I hadn't felt quite myself for quite some time. I hadn't been sleeping well and was experiencing headaches, stomachaches, and dizziness. The pace at which I was living my life was intense. The pressures I'd put on myself could only find their way out of my mind and body when I held still, which was mainly when I slept, and I hadn't done that much in the past year. I was a doer, and I hated being at rest. I felt viable and valuable when I was *doing*. In fact, I had perfected the art of living as a "human doing"; I didn't know how to simply be a "human being."

That day, I ignored my stress and went to work at Bryan Hospital to do what I knew best and what had always made me feel better: serve others. By 1:30 in the afternoon, I was nauseous, dizzy, and had a severe headache. I walked out of my office and told my assistant I was going to get some medicine from the employee health nurse. When I arrived at the nurse's office, she took my blood pressure, then immediately told me she would be taking me to the emergency department. She put me in a wheelchair and took me down the hall to the elevator. We sped through the door of the hospital's emergency facility, and before I knew it, I was lying in a hospital bed surrounded by medical staff.

Someone put a pill under my tongue and people were scurrying around me. "It's a heart attack," I thought with surprise and caught my breath. What would Scott and the boys do if I didn't make it? I felt stunned and helpless. But there was one thing I *could* do as I lay there at the mercy of the health care providers buzzing around me. I did what always brought me peace. I began talking with God.

"Okay, God, if it's my time to go, please take care of my sons and my husband. Let them know how much I love them and help my family deal with this in a way that won't be damaging to them." In my spirit, I sensed a message coming back: "Be still and know I am God." It sounded like good advice to me, so I settled back into the crisp white pillows and relaxed my body, allowing my doctors and nurses to do their job.

In the end, I learned there had been no heart attack. Months of tests revealed everything was fine with me physically, but my brain still was nearly constantly foggy and I was always sleepy. I continued to have stomachaches and headaches—and felt as if I was choking. I wanted to hide from the world, and I didn't enjoy the things in life that I usually enjoyed.

As a last resort, I contacted a psychologist friend, Dr. Maria, and asked if I could see her. If my body was fine, there had to be something going on in my mind. After several visits and assessments, Dr. Maria diagnosed me with post traumatic stress disorder (PTSD) and major depressive disorder (MDD). I was surprised, but relieved. At least now there was an explanation for the physical and emotional ache I had been feeling. What I was suffering had a name.

But really. PTSD? In my mind, this ailment was strongly linked to the violence and fear soldiers experience during times of war. I hadn't been in any wars. How could I have PTSD? Talking with Dr. Maria, who specialized in refugee and immigrant trauma, I learned immigrants and refugees are even more likely to develop PTSD and MDD than military personnel.

Leaving one's homeland creates dissonance for all individuals. Dr. Maria's research had uncovered the fact that age of displacement makes a difference on the person's identity development. If an individual left their birth country before Age 10, they most often saw themselves as a person of the new land with the heritage of their birth country. If the individual left after age 18, that individual will always consider themselves as a person from their birth country living in a new place.

This is where it becomes really interesting. If you leave your homeland somewhere between ages 10 and 18, when your identity is being shaped, you are especially vulnerable and may live in a state of dissonance most of your life when it comes to finding a sense of belonging. Your identity can take decades to solidify when you are a "third culture kid" (TCK). This is a term given to children who live a life that includes going back and forth between two or more cultures.

But just because you live between cultures doesn't mean you will have PTSD and/or depression. The real challenges come when there's turmoil and no support. That combination is the perfect recipe for PTSD, as Dr. Maria helped me understand. My experiences as a young immigrant without my parents, during the Iran hostage crisis, and the challenges that happened after that, were traumatic and had not been ever resolved internally.

The constant question in my own mind after I had been in the United States for a while was whether I was Iranian or American. As most immigrants are, I was pressured both indirectly and directly to assimilate and to do it quickly. In my mind that meant giving up part of myself and becoming "American." I believed remaining safe meant fitting in. But it's impossible to give up what you can't change about yourself. Back then, and in many ways even now, it is "safer" to fit in than to stand out, but safe is not authentic. This conflict existed in me until I began to process the traumas I had experienced.

I slowly began to realize that, just because I left Iran at the age of 12 doesn't mean I'm not Iranian anymore. It's a part of me and always will be. And I'm *also* American, because I've been in this country 4 decades. Now I realize I'm both, and it's okay to be both.

I hear people ask, "Why does a person have to be identified as one thing or another, or both?" It's because you are what you are. My father's words when we arrived for the first time in England had always stuck with me: "You may be the only Iranian these people will ever meet. Make sure you represent your country and your family well." I also had taken to heart my mother's constant reminder: "You are a woman with a deep heritage from a people who are strong and courageous. You must be an educated woman who can stand up and be respected."

But by the time I received the diagnosis of PTSD and MDD, I had been an American citizen for more than 15 years and had intentionally built, with Scott, what I truly believed to be a happy life in the United States. I had no idea this was creating dissonance within me. But one thing was clear after my trip to the emergency room: the pain was real and I needed to keep digging for clarity, keep trying to understand and uncover answers so I could get healthy.

I agreed to regular therapy with Dr. Maria. I began to address some of the pain I'd lived with for so long that had grown within me until it was unbearable:

- It had been painful to leave Iran at the age of 12 to go to England—even though it also had been very exciting. Leaving my family in Iran was deeply painful.
- It had truly been devastating to come to America at 15, be left in a boarding school, live through fear for my family and friends after the Iranian crisis, which continues even today, become the butt of others' jokes because I was Iranian, and continuously hear, "You don't belong here."
- I experienced 32 moves by the age of 40, having to start anew each time. I had been separated for years from family, then for months at a time from my husband, who was out to sea with the Navy.
- I had suffered two miscarriages and the deaths of many loved ones, including several close family members in Iran.
- The most painful death of all had been the loss of my beloved Ahga. As I worked through these many painful experiences, it became clear I had never really let my dad go emotionally.

■ To make matters worse, I had taken on the burdens of making something of myself, not only to make my parents proud, but to prove to others that I am smart, hard-working, and dedicated to not being a burden on society, which I believed was what most people believed about immigrants. No matter how much I accomplished, how much money I made, how many awards I was given, I didn't believe I was good enough, so I was trapped in a constant effort to prove myself and most importantly to find a feeling of belonging in this land.

It was simply all more than I could handle physically and emotionally.

It's not that I hadn't tried hard to cope. When bad things happened, as they do in everyone's life, I hadn't allowed myself to grieve and process the pain. Instead, I gathered up every ounce of courage and strength I could find within myself and I persevered. My mantra was, "That which does not kill me, makes me stronger." I thought this toughness was admirable, but I didn't realize it was making my pain worse. My head had dealt with life's challenges, but my heart was still in pain and I didn't know how to make it go away. There was a frightened and exhausted 15-year old girl who felt lost and alone most of the time.

Gradually, between medication, counseling sessions with Dr. Maria, rest, and many hours, days, and months of effort, I began to heal—much more slowly than this "doing" body liked, but I could feel the healing taking place. I learned that I needed to *be still* long enough to process the things that had happened to me. Multiple times, when I prayed, I sensed God saying, "Let it go!" And so I did. I slowly began to release the pain and the need to prove myself, which launched me on a journey of transformation that continues still today.

I learned to let my mind and heart make peace with each other. With the help and encouragement of family and close friends, I learned to accept me. I learned to love the 15-year old girl. To hear her. To tend to her needs. To understand that her voice matters. I came to the conclusion that human beings are made for connection and to be authentically connected to others begins with authentic connection with oneself. I am deeply connected to my family and ancestors in Iran. I am also deeply connected to my family and friends in this country. When I'm at my best, I feel these connections at my core, and I have a deep love for humanity, for people from all walks of life.

Sometimes, as all humans do, I push away connections with others. Sometimes disconnection happens because I am fearful of acceptance. My experiences taught me that being "normal" meant fitting in. But fitting in shouldn't mean giving up parts of ourselves. We don't live in an either/or world. We live in a and/both world. We are better when we *genuinely* enjoy the complex and multidimensional parts of each other. I've come to realize that peace begins to unfold inside each of us when we sense we are accepted for all parts of us. When we find the courage to truly understand ourselves and one another, no matter how difficult, to savor our differences, we are supporting the authentic development in each other. That is the gift of and/both.

I believe my pain and struggle have blessed me with powerful lessons, and so I have continued to research and teach from the lessons of inclusion and leadership, and to spread this message to as many people as I can. I believe the fact that I am an immigrant who has overcome painful experiences makes it possible for me to help others like me and those who live and work with them. To do this, we must be willing to be vulnerable and authentic, as I finally was with Dr. Maria's help. We must be willing to share our stories, listen to others' stories, embrace our pain and struggle, and grow together.

*   *   *

Butterflies go through four stages of life: egg, larva (caterpillar), pupa, and adult insect. When the larva is fully grown, it stops feeding and begins to search for a place to transform into a pupa. Some spin a cocoon after attaching themselves to a leaf or twig, but most simply hang from their chosen spot and allow the process of metamorphosis to begin.

The inside of a pupa is a place of destruction. The larva releases enzymes that destroy many of the body's tissues. Some of the creature's organs stay intact and others, such as muscles, become broken down into clumps of cells. Some of the cells can be reused and some create what is called "imaginal discs," the precursors of adult body parts.

In other words, the butterfly or moth larva actually digests itself, tearing down the structure of its body before it releases hormones that begin to build the parts back into the beautiful insect we know and love.

This provides a good metaphor for human struggles. Like the butterfly's body, the human body is built to grow and change as the result of the struggles we experience individually throughout our lives. We even see this phenomenon in physical training. Working out at the gym tears down old tissue, and then, with time, rest and stretching builds new tissue to make the body noticeably stronger.

Emotional maturity can't happen without struggle, either. The feelings, thoughts, and actions we experience during crisis can help us grow in positive ways, such as increasing our knowledge, improving our resilience and stamina, and giving us an ability to open our hearts to people who are different from us, to become more perceptive of their experiences, and needs.

We often look back on our struggles and wish they hadn't happened. We find ourselves avoiding situations that might require us to struggle. In fact, our tendency is to want to protect our children from struggle. We may think we need to swoop in and solve the problems of those we love, so they don't have to experience pain. We may be tempted to take over and do the hard work for them. However, when we do that, we are literally robbing them of the opportunity to grow into their beautiful selves.

If a butterfly chrysalis is split open to help the insect emerge, metamorphosis cannot be completed. The insect can't continue to develop outside of the chrysalis, so early emergence stunts their growth. When a butterfly is released early from a chrysalis, it is unformed and unable to fly, perhaps dying soon after its release. Our intention may have been to help it, but in reality, it struggles more after emergence because the chrysalis has not been allowed to fully complete its transformation. The same substance that breaks down the body of a pupa fills and expands the wings of the full-grown adult.

The lesson of this metaphor is not that we should abandon one another through our struggles, but that we should support each other without interfering too much as we are going through our own personal processes of painful transformation. When I was experiencing my struggles after the diagnosis of PTSD and MDD, I received support from many people: my husband and children, physicians, friends, my faculty mentor for my master's degree, former coworkers, and friends from church. They came alongside me and helped me with a variety of things—in so many ways I could never list them all. Their support became a scaffolding to help me through the process, but the struggle was still mine to go through.

As time went on, like the pupa in the chrysalis, I began to put the pieces back together, further growing and developing through past and present events in my life, including helping the Filipino nurses learn about American culture, helping immigrants and refugees settle in my hometown, and taking in an exchange student from South Korea who came to live with us in 2005. I started looking at my struggles in a different way. The pain had been worth it, I thought, if it meant I could be a part of making our world a better place.

I emerged from my dark and painful chrysalis into a life of deeper meaning and renewed hope.

* * *

After receiving the diagnosis of PTSD and MDD, I had to stop doing everything, and allow myself time to heal from what I now understood as devastating losses that resulted in some deep emotional wounds. So, I resigned my full-time position at Bryan Hospital. It was not easy to let go, because I loved my work and I didn't want to let others down, but I knew if I remained on the same path, my health would continue to decline. I also put my master's degree on hold. I had been working on it slowly, taking one class at a time since 2003, through Doane University. I later returned and completed my degree, receiving a special award for persevering through hardship and finishing.

As I continued regular therapy sessions with Dr. Maria, I found that I would need more than just quiet time to find my way back. I needed something to look forward to, to keep my brain working—a way to share what I had learned. I needed to do something that would not only fulfill my desire to help others but also help me. Dr. Maria and I talked through many possibilities, and the idea that emerged was teaching.

I had done a great deal of teaching and curriculum development in my career in human resources. I gained energy when I watched others learn and grow. Developing the potential in other human beings filled me with great joy and purpose. Before I left Bryan hospital, I had been asked to create and teach a course in cultural diversity to students at Bryan College of Health Sciences. After a while, the idea of creating a course about cultural diversity for future health practitioners seemed like the perfect way to continue my passion and build on what I'd been doing prior to this health challenge.

* * *

Since 1992, the more I came into contact with people who were having difficulty navigating differences, the more I could see myself bridging that gap and helping others do the same. The seed of this vision was planted in me the day the nurse had berated my father for not "learning English." At first, my anger motivated a desire to prove to her and everyone else that there was a positive way of approaching these challenges.

But since then, I had learned much about human motivation, fear of ambiguity, and anxiety that comes with feeling incompetent, especially in life and death situations. I'd learned to be curious about the why behind someone's behavior instead of allowing it to emotionally hijack me and put me on the defensive. I thought of the incident with the nurse in a much different way.

I wanted to teach others what I'd learned, and that's one of the reasons I implemented a diversity and cultural competence initiative in a health care system that was mostly homogenous. I also wanted to come alongside others who were doing the same thing in other places and tell them to hang in there. To encourage and support them. To let them know that this hard work does indeed have the power to transform people, organizations, and communities. Mostly, on a personal level, I desperately wanted to make sure no one else was humiliated the way my father and I were on that day.

I recognized that teaching in an academic setting and working as a consultant most likely would require a doctoral degree. An application to a doctoral program requires the applicant to identify a topic that eventually will become the theme of a doctoral dissertation. Specifically, doctoral candidates are encouraged to think of a question upon which their dissertation can be based. The question becomes a homing device throughout the process of research and writing.

I began thinking about what was missing in the landscape of diversity in health care. I asked myself what big questions remained for me in my own life surrounding diversity and health care disparities. I did indeed have one gigantic nagging question that kept popping into my mind: "How can we ensure health care situations lead to results more like the one involving the 12-year-old Native American boy and less like the situation with my dad?"

I believed if I could understand the answer to that question, I could help health care workers develop the internal capacity to create lasting systemic changes in health care. But I knew I couldn't find the answer without extensive research.

For my doctoral program, I chose the University of Nebraska–Lincoln's PhD in human sciences with specialization in leadership for two reasons. First, I would be allowed to tailor my coursework to meet my research interest. Because I was interested in diversity, cultural competence, inclusion, and leadership, I could take a wide variety of courses, from a variety of departments: anthropology, organizational behavior, leadership, psychology, and public health.

The second reason I chose the University of Nebraska was Dr. Gina Matkin. Her personal passion and research also related to diversity, inclusion, and cultural competence. And she also believed in the impact of developmental levels using the same assessment I had worked with, the IDI. She would be the perfect person to mentor and guide my research.

Then the other shoe dropped.

Questions

1. What part of your life would benefit from you being courageous? What would that look like?
2. What part of your life would benefit from you demonstrating more humility? What would that look like?
3. How can you apply the responses to the above questions to your continued growth in creating inclusion in your organization, school, community, or place of worship?
4. In what ways are you vulnerable with yourself to admit what your needs and struggles are? How can you address these to avoid consequences like burnout and depression?

9

The Rewards of Struggle

Go learn a lesson of the flowers;
Joy's season is in life's young spring,
Then seize, like them, the fleeting hours.

—A. J. Arbery

I had been sick with a cough and cold that wouldn't go away. I kept thinking I just needed more time to heal. But I was always so tired. I dismissed it as part of the PTSD and MDD, and I was determined to power through it (obviously I still had more to learn about listening to my body). I had promised Scott I would go see the doctor after I took the GMAT (the last part of my application for the PhD program), so I went to our doctor's walk-in clinic the afternoon after the test. He diagnosed me with pneumonia.

After a 10-day round of antibiotics and a 3-day round of antibiotic infusions, I was admitted to the hospital because I wasn't getting better. On January 18, I had a CT scan of my lungs. The next day was Dr. Martin Luther King Jr. Day and as my husband and I were watching the inauguration of President Obama, a physician walked into my hospital room to share the results of the CT scan.

Becoming Inclusive, pages 111–124
Copyright © 2021 by Information Age Publishing
All rights of reproduction in any form reserved.

I had a mass on my pancreas that had woven itself around my spleen. I had two options: biopsy the mass or go ahead and do the surgery to remove it. Either way, I would need to see a specialist. Scott and I did not know how to make a decision like that.

"If I was your sister," I asked the doctor, "what would you recommend I do and who would you recommend do it?"

"I'd recommend removing it due to the size and location," he answered, "and I would recommend seeing Dr. Are, a specialist at University of Nebraska Medical Center."

Now I was facing not only the psychological challenges related to PTSD and MDD, but recovery from pneumonia and possible cancer. Scott and I were in shock. But we also were both in an odd place of peace. Maybe it was because we were feeling a hopeful glow from the inauguration of this country's first Black president. Maybe it was because we already had gone through and recovered from so much in our lives that we believed it would be okay in the end. Whatever it was, that feeling sustained us and helped us make plans for all the necessary steps to address this unknown.

After Scott left the hospital, I turned to the source that always comforts me: my faith. I sat with my Bible on my lap, talking to God. I opened the Bible, not looking for any particular passage, and the first words I saw were, "Jesus said to the woman your faith has saved you. Go in peace."

I read the words over and over again, eventually falling asleep with the book still open in my lap. The next morning, when the nurse came in to change the calendar, I asked if I could have the page she'd just torn off.

"Yesterday was a day that will go down in history for me personally, and the calendar page is like a souvenir," I said. "I fell asleep with the Bible opened to a page that confirmed all my hard work has been worth it."

I still have that page. It hangs on the dream board in my office.

A second CT scan showed I had a 4.5 cm × 4 cm mass. It was mucinous, and if it was not cancer then it potentially could become cancer later. The doctor recommended surgery as soon as possible to remove the mass and ⅓ of my pancreas, my spleen, and 2 lymph nodes on my stomach. The anesthesiologist wanted my lungs to get stronger first, so surgery had to be delayed until March 16th. Scott and I looked at one another with amazement. The tumor would be removed on the exact day I had become a U.S. citizen 17 years earlier!

We arrived at the University of Nebraska Medical Center at 4:00 a.m. I had quite an entourage. My baby sister had flown in from New York and she went with us to the hospital, along with our sons and some friends. Dr. Are told us it would be a long surgery (5 to 6 hours) and that recovery would be grueling. Boy was he right! I was in the hospital for 6 days and at home recovering for 3 months.

On the fourth day of hospitalization, my cell phone rang. Dr. Gina Matkin was calling to interview me for the PhD program. We talked for a while, and at the end of our conversation she said, "Congratulations, Helen. I want to be the first person to officially welcome you to the program." I was elated. I had yet to hear results of the lab test on the mass. But, still, I was thrilled that I had been accepted into a PhD program.

Yes, I'd had my share of other successes over the years. I finished my master's degree with a 4.0 grade point average and won the Keith Berlage award for perseverance. Before that, in 2004, I was given a key to the city by the Mayor of Lincoln for my contributions to advancing the dreams of Dr. Martin Luther King Jr. in our community. I had won a Tribute to Women Award in 2005, a prestigious award that had been given by the YWCA to women in Lincoln for 3 decades. But being accepted to a PhD program, for me, was really something special. Me, the person who had for so long believed I was stupid because school kids in England made fun of the way I spoke English and the kids at Florida Central Academy had made me feel like an oddball.

Whether I would be able to finish or even begin my degree program was still unknown. But I had been accepted and that was a victory in and of itself.

Before Gina hung up, I asked her what advice she had for me, a nontraditional student, as to how to succeed in the PhD program. She had pursued her PhD while in a relationship and working full-time, so she understood where my question was coming from. She said, "Two things will help you. One, make a space at home that brings you positive energy, so you are excited to study and work. And two, appreciate the journey. Don't lose focus on today by looking too far into the future." Those two bits of advice continue to serve me even now.

On Sunday, March 22nd, Dr. Are and his team walked into my hospital room, where I was surrounded by family and friends, and told me *I did not have cancer*. Much cheering and high fiving ensued. It sounded as though Nebraska had made a touchdown! People were celebrating all around me and I laid there, overwhelmed, with tears of joy rolling down my face.

Later that evening, I tried to capture in my journal the overwhelming gratitude and humility I felt after having gone through all of this:

Now, here I sit today by the window sobbing. I don't know what is causing me to cry. I think a deep sense of gratitude. I don't want to feel guilty that I have been spared from pancreatic cancer; yet I do. And, because I have been spared, I want to continue the rest of my days always seeking you first, oh God. I want more than anything to trust in you. I want to love graciously and generously the people you put in my path. To give and serve others because you've called us to love others as we love ourselves.

Memories of that day still create such a deep sense of gratitude that it almost always brings me to tears. It explains why I have continued to work toward helping create a society that values human differences AND people with the skills to work toward it. I felt a change in myself.

I have to admit, the pain in my heart was still there, but now I knew what it was. Now I could work with it and integrate it into my life. In fact, I suddenly realized it was *because* of all that pain and my opportunity to overcome it that I was becoming a better version of myself. I was emerging from the darkness with new skills, a new understanding—and a new personal strength.

The pain had given me the gift of resilience and freed me from a feeling that I was not in control of what was happening to me. I began to believe in myself and my ability to come through dark times. I began to approach difficulty with a new mantra: "I can face this. I've done harder things before." Memories of the many difficult things I had gone through during my life were becoming powerful reminders I could draw on anytime I needed them.

Because of the pain I had endured for so many years, I now had a direction for my life and a crystal-clear vision of how I could help others. I had answered the nagging question about myself that had run through everything I attempted in the world of diversity. I could open up to people, tell them my story, maybe develop new ways to promote acculturation, and contribute to a body of work that might one day help our world experience a beautiful metamorphosis.

All of the little dreams I had kept at the back of my heart were now becoming real.

And that was the beautiful reward of my struggle.

*　*　*

My personal mindset was changing as it was shaped by experience and education. But what was research revealing about the connection between experience and developmental shifts in human beings? Could we discover how we might be able to enhance our ability to connect across cultural differences (not just race, ethnicity, religion, and nationality). In the early

2000s, researchers beyond Milton Bennet and Mitch Hammer were exploring this question.

Ayas' mixed method study of third-year medical students found there was no relationship between international experience and changes in perceived developmental levels of intercultural sensitivity. But participants agreed that active participation, reflection and dialogue, and open mindedness, were a few of the factors related to effective intercultural experience (Ayas, 2006).

Lundgren's study, exploring the developmental process of teachers, indicated that professional development experiences are enhanced through cohorts of learners (people learning together in groups), especially school-based cohorts with administrative support (Lundgren, 2007).

In Moodian's study, participants' developmental levels of intercultural sensitivity actually declined between two assessments (as some of our participants' assessments did at Bryan College). Moodian explained that there may be a correlation between stress and decreased intercultural sensitivity, and that could have been a factor in the participants' developmental level (Moodian, 2009).

Li studied a group of Canadian health care executives. The executives were highly motivated leaders, but they were not able to make progress in intercultural sensitivity development on a personal or organizational level. Li found that the executives actually accumulated *more fear* after IDI assessment and training (Li, 2010).

What does this mean? In part, it's a caution for us to realize that, while experience is a valuable teacher, experience alone is not enough to cause a shift in the development of intercultural sensitivity. It is rather *whether and how meaning is given* to the experience.

As individuals grow in an intercultural mindset, they recognize the complexity of culture and how deeply rooted it is in their own lives. However, the ability to *create meaning* from experiences with diverse populations progresses only as a person's developmental level increases (Bennett, 1986). The ability to advance in personal development is not marked by *what* you think about an intercultural situation but by *how* you think about that experience.

Christopher and Hickinbottom (2008) stressed that individuals will be "doomed to being narrow and ethnocentric as long as they remain unaware of the cultural assumptions underlying their work" (p. 565). For me, this realization changed the underlying motivation of my doctoral work from curiosity to necessity. If we don't want to be doomed to a narrow, ethnocentric view of our world and all the misunderstanding, conflict—even violence—it inevitably will lead to, we must all become aware of our own cultural assumptions.

I attended the training to become a qualified IDI administrator in the Spring of 2007. When I took the assessment that time, I found out I was in the level of acceptance. That was an improvement over minimization, but I also discovered I was holding on to issues related to my identity as a multicultural human being that negatively influenced my frame of reference for what was happening globally. It was an election year, and the rhetoric from those running for office included Iran, once again. The anguish of what could happen was and continues to be a very real, painful part of my daily existence.

I was beginning to really grasp the importance of developmental mindset as an antecedent to cultural competence and inclusive mindset. During the 3-day IDI training, I had the opportunity to learn from Dr. Mitch Hammer and Dr. Michael Paige, along with one of Dr. Paige's students, Dr. Akiko Maeker. I quickly realized that Akiko, a Japanese American married to a White American male as I was, could relate to what I was thinking and experiencing. So we had lunch and shared a little of our life stories. We were both mothers of two sons (though hers were much younger than mine), and we both saw the importance of mindset shift in individuals. We both had studied and were excited about the power of coaching (as defined by the International Coaching Federation) to help individuals grow. I had no idea how much that lunch encounter and conversation with Akiko would impact me as I entered my PhD program.

I loved the idea of the IDI assessment. It was exciting to know there was a highly valid and reliable psychometric assessment that could measure people's mindsets around difference (where a person falls on Bennett's DMIS model). Mostly, I loved knowing the assessment could help people grow. Any group—academic, governmental, corporate, or other—can use this assessment to help improve communication and interaction between its members. I thought, what an important and inspiring tool this will be in many different contexts.

I saw this firsthand when I used the assessment at Bryan College. When the college asked me to develop and teach a course on diversity and cultural competence I agreed, but only if I could use the IDI to assess the students' ability to give meaning to cultural differences they experienced. The college president agreed. In fact, the college had launched a formal strategic initiative to grow students' level of intercultural competence from entrance to graduation, and the president believed the IDI could help measure the initiative's success. Her ultimate goal was to enhance the college's course offerings for students and provide training for faculty and staff.

The dean of students, dean of nursing, and dean of allied health were instrumental in developing an implementation plan for this collegewide initiative. The dean of students had a strong interest in and commitment to intercultural sensitivity development and volunteered to spearhead the initiative.

I began with the students in my class. As I worked with them, using the IDI to measure and develop their level of intercultural sensitivity, they repeatedly asked if faculty and staff were being taught this information also. When I said no, they asked why not. I shared the students' concerns with college leaders, and they agreed faculty and staff should take the IDI and learn where they stood. This was a pivotal moment in the life of Bryan College and it has changed the culture of the college, thus powerfully impacting the graduates, as well as their faculty and staff.

As I thought about what I knew about positive psychology, I began wondering what would cause a person to want to move along the continuum represented by the IDI scale. What is the underlying psychological state necessary? What goes on inside of a person's mind and heart that makes change possible?

I had become aware that I *needed* to change and earnestly began *wanting* to change at that moment when I realized my frustration with the nurse in my dad's hospital room had as much to do with how I reacted as it did what she said. In contrast, I thought about Bryan's chaplain and his culturally competent mindset as demonstrated with the boy who died after getting hit by a car. Is there a way to help people like the nurse and me to change so we can be more like the chaplain? If so, what is that way?

These questions formed the basis of my PhD research and the topic of my dissertation. The time I already had spent working in diversity, inclusion, and cultural competence had provided me with a few clues.

* * *

Scott and my sons had yet to meet any of my extended family from Iran. I had been asked multiple times to come visit, but never felt the timing was right, mostly because of my faith. I had become a Christian and most of my family were Muslim. I didn't know what they would think or how they would react, and I didn't feel I could bear the uneasiness—or utter conflict—it might cause.

Then, in 2009, the opportunity came for us to attend a family reunion in Turkey with the members of my mother's side of the family. So, we did it. My uncle had rented a villa in the ancient city of Silivri, just outside of Istanbul along the Sea of Marmara, where the whole family would gather.

It was the first time I had traveled internationally with Scott, Jonathan, and Alan. Each of us had gone on mission trips overseas individually, and I'd traveled to multiple places for work, but this was our first family trip abroad. Jonathan was 23, and had just finished a bachelor's degree in audio engineering and entertainment business. Alan was 19, and had just finished his freshman year of college.

My grandmother, my mom's mother, Naneh Shahree, was 83 years old and so looking forward to meeting my sons and husband! I had visited her while she was in England in 2006, and she had said proudly to me then, "I have grandchildren who live in different countries and don't speak the same language as me. That makes me an international grandmother, right?" Prior to that trip in 2006, the last time I had seen my grandmother was when we visited Iran for the last time in the Summer of 1978. I had promised her then that I would do everything I could to make sure at least one of my four grandparents got to meet my kids and husband.

When we arrived at the Silivri villa by taxi, some of my family from Iran, England, and Malaysia were already there. We laughed and cried and embraced one another, wondering why we had waited so long. It was a gathering filled with many emotions for all of us.

As we arrived, all the men gathered on Scott's side of the taxi and began welcoming him and our sons with kisses on the cheek and robust hugs. Later than evening, as we lay in bed, I asked Scott what he thought about that. After our wedding day, he had said he allowed my father to kiss him on the cheek out of respect, but if either of my brothers or any other male family member ever tried it he would lay them out!

His answer to my question in Turkey still sticks with me: "Just because I'm okay with it here, doesn't mean I am any less of a man or an American. Like your dad told *you* when you were a girl, I may be the only American man they ever meet. I want to represent my country and our family well."

I fell in love with Scott even more in that moment. And my desire for research grew even more. I wanted to understand how it could be that he had changed so much. When I married him, he would sing the words to the song by the band Alabama, "My baby is American made, born and bred in the USA," as a matter of pride, and on the day of our wedding he had felt threatened by a Middle Eastern tradition he didn't understand. How had he grown and developed as a human being to become *this* kind of man who accepts such a very un-American tradition as men kissing each other on the cheek? He isn't perfect. But he is inclusive. He has an intercultural mindset. How does that happen?

When we were waiting for our plane to head home from Istanbul, I asked my sons if being there helped them understand their mother better. Our oldest, Jonathan, said, "Mom, it makes me understand *myself* better." Wow! What a wonderful gift. Nothing I could have purchased for either of them as a souvenir of that special time with our family could make up for the gift of self-awareness and self-confidence they gained.

Both Jonathan and Alan left Turkey frustrated that I hadn't taught them to speak Farsi. While everyone (except my grandmother and a few aunts) spoke English, my sons wanted to speak Farsi. In that moment, I realized how much things had changed. My sons' desire to learn Farsi is something I never imagined as a young adult in the United States when I was trying so hard to "fit in" and hide my identity.

This realization would impact me greatly during the years ahead. The trip to Turkey also made me realize that family bonds are the same across national and linguistic boundaries. Family bonds among the people of all nations and races are strong, even between family members who haven't ever met.

When we returned from Turkey, I started my PhD program. It was time for me to put my money where my mouth was—an English idiom that always makes me laugh as I visualize lifting a fistful of dollars to my open mouth. I was very excited to begin researching in earnest and find answers to the burning questions related to cultural competence that had filled my mind for so many years, through so many difficult and perplexing challenges.

My program chair, Gina, was instrumental in helping me create and implement a program. I can't say enough about how important the guidance of a nonjudgmental, encouraging program chair is on the successful completion of a PhD program.

Gina's willingness to help me learn and grow, while challenging me to always think about the big picture, helped us form a bond that continues still today. We joke that we are sisters from different motherlands, different religions, different sexual orientations—yet we are sisters. There is enough similarity (not sameness) between us that we have been able to bond, and yet there are enough differences between us that we have challenged one another and have grown.

Three classes are considered full time in the graduate program at UNL. But because of my recent surgery and the course I was teaching at Bryan College of Health Sciences, I decided to take just two classes each semester. In my first class, "Theoretical Foundations of Leadership," we studied leadership from Lao Zu and Wéber to Stogdil and Bennis, exploring a multitude of modern theories of leadership such as transformational, authentic, and servant leadership, to name a few.

The professor began the first class by asking, "What did you do this summer, and why did you choose this PhD program?" I responded with an account of the surgery and recovery, our trip to Turkey and the question I wanted to research. During break that evening, the professor pulled me to the side, congratulated me on being in class and encouraged me to speak up during his classes. He explained that I was the most experienced (aka oldest) in the class, and he knew others would be able to learn much from my experiences.

That class and that semester helped me gain a broader understanding of the scientific research that has explored the topics of leadership, leaders, and followers. I had served as a community and organization leader in multiple places, but I hadn't studied leadership the way this class forced me to. We had to read eight to ten peer-reviewed research articles every week, write a review about each one, and come to class prepared to engage in in-depth discussion with our peers. As a result, leadership became one of the most important focuses of my research.

In her book *Dare to Lead,* Dr. Brené Brown (2018) says, "Studying leadership is way easier than leading" (n.p.). I wholeheartedly agree, and I believe it is that way with any topic. I entered academia after nearly 3 decades of working and volunteering in industry. I had led programs, initiatives, and people. But I hadn't ever thought of myself as a leader. I always thought of myself simply as a person who was called to serve others.

It wasn't until I began to study leadership that I began to see why others saw me as a leader. Neither title, nor power, nor money makes one a leader. In his book *Leadership Theory and Practice,* Dr. Peter Northouse (2013) explains that there are as many definitions of leadership as there are people trying to describe leadership.

The definition Kevin Cashman (2017) uses in his book *Leadership From the Inside Out* deeply resonates with me. He says, "Leadership is authentic influence that creates value" (p. 4).

Leaders are found in many different places, entrenched in many different disciplines, with many different goals. Leaders who wrestle with the issues of diversity can be leaders of families, classes, or book clubs—as well as leaders of multibillion-dollar corporations and entire countries. Every leader at every level has some of the same concerns, and those who are successful in their dealings with diversity have some of the same qualities and skills regardless of the size or nature of the group they lead.

* * *

I conducted the IDI assessments with faculty and staff at Bryan College of Health Sciences in May of 2010. They met with me first in a group to learn how results are interpreted, and then each person met with me privately to understand their individual results and come up with a plan for their own development.

When it came to faculty and staff, I recommended that several key individuals should go through the IDI training first to better understand the instrument and decide how to advance efforts at the college. The dean of students and two faculty members attended the training before everyone else. This created extra momentum for implementing even more collegewide initiatives. A diversity advisory committee was created, made up of leaders from the community. A new faculty and staff diversity council was established, and diversity-related educational requirements for faculty and staff were increased.

As more faculty and staff became culturally competent, more students were willing and able to increase their own cultural competence. After 2010, the IDI-measured developmental scores of graduating students at Bryan College increased in small increments every year. The scores supported research that indicates individuals cannot grow others' level of intercultural sensitivity to a level they themselves haven't reached (Bennett, 2004; Long, 2012).

In May 2013, all Bryan College faculty and staff took the IDI for a second time. Group results were shared again, and anyone who was interested met with me to discuss changes in their individual assessment. The results surprised us. All faculty and staff had embarked on the same developmental process, but individual results varied. As measured by the IDI, some individuals' developmental level of intercultural sensitivity (DO) increased, some stayed the same, and some decreased.

What happened? Why didn't everyone experience an increase? I believed if we could explain this, we would have clues as to how we might, as a society and world, learn to change ourselves.

* * *

Research using the IDI states that a majority of the population (around 60%) falls into minimization, which was surprising to me when I began this work. In my career and research, I've assessed over 9,000 people from multiple walks of life. My research also shows—as IDI research has shown—that most people are in the minimization level. They have a desire to create workplaces, communities, or educational institutions where the differences between people who report to them aren't stumbling blocks to success but instead lead to enhanced synergy.

However, most people in minimization want me to tell them "everything they need to know" about a specific group and how to make their team more inclusive or innovative. They want it to be simple. They want a quick fix for diversity, inclusion, and cultural competence, so they can move forward with their goals. Minimization in and of itself is not bad. It is just not enough when it comes to building inclusive workplaces, schools, and communities.

Why do most people fall into minimization? My theory is that is because we have widely taught that equal treatment is fair treatment. Even our legal system follows that rule. In the mid-1980s, as a young human resources professional, I attended an EEOC (Equal Employment Opportunity Commission) training. An attorney who was doing part of the training said, "I don't care if you lock up your employees in the closet and beat them every day as long as you do the *same* way to ALL of your employees regardless of race, ethnicity, national origin, religion, or age." (Note that disabilities did not become a protected class until the American Disabilities Act of 1990.) This is an example of the idea that equal treatment is fair treatment.

In recent years, we have seen a desirable shift towards *equi*table treatment instead of equal treatment. Equitable treatment takes into consideration the *different* things people need in order to get to the same goal. People's needs are different because they have been influenced by many different cultural inputs. However, it probably will be decades before the idea of equitable treatment becomes part of the fabric of our culture.

The other reason I believe humanity tends to fall into minimization is because of our history with assimilation (pressure to "become like us"). Since the early years of this nation's history, we've wanted those in the minority to be, act, think, talk, behave, and believe like those of the majority who are "in power." We did this with the original residents of this land, and we have done it with others since then. Each generation has forced assimilation in its own way.

This new century is challenging us to think differently. Can we walk alongside newcomers to this land as they adapt? Can we be the scaffolding they need to learn how to succeed at life here, instead of the zapper that zaps them for being different? Better yet, can we just be accepting of differences and recognize that magic happens when differences are celebrated? We teach children in school to be brave and stand out. To appreciate the uniqueness in their friends. When do we lose this perspective as adults?

Quick fixes for diversity, inclusion, and cultural competence don't exist. In fact, most of my students grow more than leaders I've worked with because students are willing to take the time needed and do the work. They know their grade is dependent on doing the developmental work I've laid out for them.

Leaders have so many demands on their time and no personal skin in the game, so they don't prioritize growth in cultural competence as a necessity for their success as leaders. It's easy to believe we already know what we need to know to lead people. It's easy to forget human beings are the most complex beings on the planet and that no amount, quality or type of information will work with all people all the time.

Due to the complexity of the human brain, human experiences, and the external factors that impact them, inclusion doesn't happen until each person is willing to embrace transformation and do the work—to struggle and earn the rewards of the struggle. Inclusion is an inside job in every person. And until individuals are held accountable for doing the hard work of development, most won't. For them, minimization is good enough to get by. For me it wasn't enough, and that's why I kept working on myself, seeking, learning, and working toward personal change. But, as I conducted more IDI assessments and coached more individuals, I began to see that the struggle isn't worth it for some people.

I took the IDI assessment again when I started the second semester of my PhD program. I was above the highest level by a few points. I was shocked and felt, again, that the assessment had to be wrong. I wondered how on earth I could have grown from acceptance to adaptation in 2 years.

Gina, who had studied with Bennett and Hammer and had become an IDI qualified administrator 2 years before me, helped me analyze and understand my personal experiences and the ways I was making meaning of them, which gave me some insight into my growth. We discussed my desire to be a bridge and help others feel valued and included and celebrate their uniqueness.

Then she reminded me that human beings never really stop changing and growing. I wasn't done transforming. She used my own words to help me realize I am *only* in adaptation. I still have lots of learning and growing to do, as everyone does.

Questions

1. What do you see as the impacts of equal treatment vs. equitable treatment in a community?
2. What are you struggling with right now? How can you make positive meaning of the struggle?
3. How can you demonstrate empathy and understanding when others face struggles?

10

Models for Change

"Patience turns stones to rubies," they say.
Yes! If you work hard and wait long, it may.

—S. M. Hafiz

O ur home in Nebraska backs up to a small section of state property
that is full of trees. We lovingly refer to it as our forest. During winter,
the trees are eerily bare. The leaves fall off when the weather turns cold in
autumn and by the time snow flies our little forest is like a boneyard, with
skeletal trees standing like sentries. Growing up on Kharg Island in southern Iran, I was not used to seeing trees lose their leaves. Though Iran is diverse in flora and fauna and does experience four seasons in some regions,
I didn't see changing seasons until I moved to England. At Stanborough
Academy in Watford, I walked through deciduous woods to get to chapel.
In the autumn, our art teacher allowed us to visit the woods and pick leaves
for projects. I loved the changing fall colors and fell in love with wandering
in the woods.

Bare winter trees are, at first glance, dull and uninteresting. In fact, they
appear dead in the right lighting, at night or on grey foggy days. But I've

Becoming Inclusive, pages 125–140
Copyright © 2021 by Information Age Publishing
All rights of reproduction in any form reserved.

often heard people say how beautiful they are. Why is this? I used to wonder how anyone could find beauty in bare trees. I now believe people see beauty there because they know what's going on inside the seemingly dead husks of those living things. They know Mother Nature is doing her work behind the scenes and they have a mental vision of the trees' lush green incarnations. They love and respect the process, even though the winter stage appears dull and uninteresting. Some even say the bare branches look like lace or the trees are like dancers in the wind.

Sadly, at first glance, we often see people as we do bare winter trees. When people behave in ways we don't understand, we sometimes assume they are bad and their actions are wrong because their actions are different from our own. We might even convince ourselves that others like them are also bad. We do this to ourselves, too. Think of the last time you made a mistake. Did you mentally kick yourself for being, saying, or doing something "stupid," all the while forgetting the wonderful things you've done and how amazing you are on the whole? This tendency is very human, and we know we should figure out how to *not* do it. But that takes some work, and we have to be willing to do the work to change our perceptions.

How can we learn to refrain from judging based only on what we see? How can we overcome our fear of the unknown and begin to celebrate one another in all our differences, in all our seasons? This has been the basis of much of my work for the last 20 years. I've been using what I discovered through all my studying, teaching, experiencing, wondering, and analyzing to try to teach others how to shift their mindsets from monocultural to intercultural. Each story, discipline, theory, and model I uncovered for myself holds some part of the answer for all of us.

The accounts of Henrietta Lacks and Tuskegee help us see how horrible it is when we get it wrong. The book *The Spirit Catches You, and You Fall Down* describes the complex challenges that get in our way and the sometimes-surprising payoff of trusting culture. Bennett and Hammer help us see our progression through stages of cultural competence using the DMIS and the IDI. Daniel Kahneman's (2013) explanation of our fast and slow brains provides insight, too, in his book *Thinking Fast and Slow*. Our fast brain is necessary for survival but works against logical, unbiased thinking. It is our slow brain (our prefrontal cortex) that allows us to be objective and move from emotional reaction to suspending judgement. Even my son's help in understanding rap music held a part of the truth for me.

It's interesting that our instinctual need to connect with others contains part of the answer to changing our perceptions of those who are different from us. Human beings were made for connection, and this primitive need motivates us continually to find new ways to connect authentically. The powerful bond of connection through family, for example, was made clear to me when we visited Turkey for the family reunion. We each are born into a family that has existed for many centuries, and we deeply love the stories we hear and tell our children about ancestors who sacrificed much for us. The intensity of those emotions can provide fuel for our desire to change—allowing us to connect more deeply with others in the world. In fact, this instinctual need that we often take for granted just might be our saving grace.

*   *   *

In health care, becoming culturally competent is an essential part of providing quality care. To make this happen in health care graduates, we spend a lot of time exposing students to people who are different from them, encouraging the students to learn about patients' different religions', nationalities', and races' perspectives of health and illness. But this may be placing the cart before the horse. I believe we first should help health care students understand the basis for growth in cultural competence—then help them grow in their own developmental mindset to acceptance as measured by the IDI. The same process can be used to guide people in other arenas of life.

Dr. Campinha-Bacote, in my opinion, has the richest and most applicable model for becoming culturally competent in health care. I really like that the very basis for her model is desire, which I equate to the developmental mindset of acceptance. The primary characteristic of acceptance is a deep understanding of one's own culture and others' cultures as a way to give meaning to differences. A person in acceptance has developed the internal capacity to suspend judgement of themselves and others and, with energy and curiosity, engage in a process to find out the "Why?" behind the behavior of the person they are interacting with.

Campinha-Bacote's Model of Cultural Competence Process (2002)

This model focuses on cultural competence as a process, requiring "health care providers to see themselves as *becoming* culturally competent rather than already being culturally competent" (p. 181).

Campinha-Bacote defines cultural competence as "the ongoing process in which the health care professional continuously strives to achieve the ability and availability to effectively work within the cultural context of the client" (p. 181).

The model offers five constructs that can help health care workers become culturally agile. These are areas of improvement anyone can access to improve a personal level of cultural agility:

- *Cultural awareness* is gained by assessing one's own biases, investigating how professional training and work has created a specific cultural lens through which we see patients, and becoming aware of discrimination in health care.
- *Cultural knowledge* is knowledge of world views of different cultural and ethnic groups.
- *Cultural skill* is the ability of the provider to do a cultural assessment (including a physical assessment) of the patient.
- *Cultural encounter* promotes face-to-face exchanges with clients from culturally diverse backgrounds. This is to encourage people to challenge their own biases about a particular cultural group and reduce the likelihood of stereotyping.
- *Cultural desire* addresses why anyone might want to engage in the process of becoming culturally aware, knowledgeable, and skillful in seeking cultural encounters.

Campinha-Bacote says:

Cultural desire is an essential component of establishing cultural competence. Without a desire to engage in the process of cultural competence, the process therefore may become fragmented at best. Lack of cultural desire may impede the ability to meet the cultural needs of others. (Montenery et al., 2013, p. e52)

I believe this aspect of cultural readiness—our desire to know one another and become better at interacting with each other, or lack of that desire—is at the heart of our ability or inability as a society to meet our diversity issues head on and overcome them. Think of it this way: When you are dating someone you truly care about, you have a deep desire to know them. You are willing to give them space to tell you what they are feeling and experiencing. You are willing to take time to really hear them, and that in part is what helps you connect and mesh your lives successfully. In diverse situations, reaching a similar level of successful interaction means being willing to be still and listen and understand the other person's world, and being willing to open ourselves—make ourselves vulnerable—to help others understand us. This is what will help us overcome our differences.

The question remains: Knowing how important desire is to overcoming diversity problems, how does one gain that desire, willingness, and cultural readiness if it's not already there? Furthermore, how can people in leadership positions explore their own desire, gain developmental readiness, embrace this model, and implement it in their organizations?

Giger and Davidhizar's Transcultural Assessment Model (2002)

This model is mostly focused on assessment of patients as unique cultural beings. The model suggests "each individual is culturally unique and should be assessed according to 6 cultural phenomena" (p. 185).

The model "builds on the seminal work of Leininger and others in space phenomena, communication, and anthropology" (Giger & Davidhizar, 2002, p. 187). Space phenomena refers to the space between two people when they communicate (see below).

- *Communication* covers every facet of communication and is considered the way culture is shared and continued. Giger and Davidhizar believe flawed communication (both verbal and non-verbal) is typically the reason for the most significant problems in working with individuals from diverse cultural backgrounds.
- *Space* refers to the distance between individuals when they interact, recognizing that all communication occurs within space. The authors follow Hall's zones of interpersonal space: intimate, personal, social and consultative, and public. They believe rules concerning personal distance vary from culture to culture and individuals have their own approach to space stemming from cultural norms. Violation of an individual's space will cause discomfort and potentially could end up influencing how the individual perceives and makes decisions regarding care.
- *Social organization* is the way a group organizes itself. "Family structure and organization, religious values and beliefs, and role assignments may all relate to ethnicity and culture" (Giger & Davidhizar, 2002, p. 185).
- *Time* is a component of interpersonal communication. The emphasis is on how different cultures approach communication when it comes to time—past, present, or future orientation. The West's future orientation to time can be a limiting factor in some patients' approach to life. A doctor easily understands why it's important to take medicine today—it improves health in the future. But someone from an Asian culture may believe the moment is more important. If a medicine has a side effect that

causes lethargy, the patient or home caregiver may believe it's not good medicine. This is what happened to Lia Lee, whose parents believed her epilepsy medicine was changing her too much in the present, so they withheld her medicine.

▪ *Environmental control* refers to the locus of control. Many people from the United States believe their locus of control is internal, meaning if they want to get better, they will go to the doctor. Much of the rest of the world believes there is an external locus of control—that God or fate is in control, and if it's their time to die no medicine will work, so seeking health care may be viewed as useless.

▪ *Biological differences* refer to genetic variations between individuals within specific racial groups; however, recognition of cultural differences between groups is most often what people point to when discussing biological differences. Giger and Davidhizar encourage health care workers to focus more on how an individual compares biologically with others in their own cultural/racial group:

> Although there is as much diversity within cultural and racial groups as there is across and among cultural and racial groups, knowledge of general baseline data relative to the specific cultural group is an excellent starting point to provide culturally appropriate care. (Giger & Davidhizar, 2002, p. 187)

* * *

I believe communication is the biggest issue that gets in our way, because it is foundational to everything else. Here is an example of why communication is so important. In 1980, Willie Ramirez was admitted to a South Florida hospital in a coma. The caregivers were told he was "intoxicado," which among Cubans means "ate or drank something bad." Hospital caregivers did not understand this linguistic difference and assumed he had taken drugs. They treated him as a drug overdose patient. In reality, he was suffering from an intracerebellar hemorrhage that continued to bleed for 2 days and resulted in Mr. Ramirez becoming quadriplegic. If caregivers can train themselves to be more aware of the likelihood of cultural differences, anticipate these differences, and ask questions before jumping to conclusions, this kind of misunderstanding might happen less often.

Even a provider's culture can complicate interaction with the patient. In the book, *Black Man in a White Coat*, Doctor Damon Tweedy (2016) says patients and families often mistake him to be an orderly when he enters a room in his white coat. However, he admits he finds himself approaching patients based on his own biases, especially when the hospital pace increases and everyone is tempted to take shortcuts.

The Giger Davidhizar model of culture competence sheds light on the cultural phenomena that make all of us different from one another. Again, this model does not address the underlying developmental readiness of the *individual* health care provider to engage in and learn about using the model for assessment of patients.

Purnell's Transcultural Assessment Model (2002)

This model originally was created as a framework for organizing cultural assessment. There are 12 cultural domains, each a piece of pie within the circle-shaped framework. The 12 domains reside within four rims inside of a circle. The outer rim represents the role of global society. The next rim represents the role of the community. The third rim depicts the role of family. And the inner rim is the individual. These rims are considered collectively to be a "metaparadigm," which means they apply broadly to the discipline of providing health care, rather than applying specifically to individual caregivers or patients.

Although the 12 domains and their concepts go from general to specific, the order in which the provider uses them can fluctuate.

- *Overview/heritage* includes concepts related to the country of origin, current residence, and the effects of the topography of the country of origin and current residence, economics, politics, reasons for emigration, educational status, and occupations.
- *Communication* includes concepts related to the dominant language and dialects; contextual use of the language; paralanguage variations such as voice volume, tone, and intonations; and the willingness to share thoughts and feelings. Important concepts include nonverbal communications such as the use of eye contact, facial expressions, touch, body language, spatial distancing practices, and acceptable greetings; temporality in terms of past, present, or future worldview orientation; clock versus social time; and the use of names.
- *Family roles and organization* includes concepts related to the head of the household and gender roles; family roles, priorities, and developmental tasks of children and adolescents; child-rearing practices; and roles of the aged and extended family members. Social status and views toward alternative lifestyles such as single

parenting, sexual orientation, childless marriages, and divorce are also included in this domain.

▪ *Workforce issues* include concepts related to autonomy, acculturation, assimilation, gender roles, ethnic communication styles, individualism, and health care practices from the country of origin.

▪ *Biocultural ecology* includes variations in ethnic and racial origins such as skin coloration and physical differences in body stature; genetic, hereditary, endemic, and topographical diseases; and differences in how the body metabolizes drugs.

▪ *High-risk behaviors* include the use of tobacco, alcohol, and recreational drugs; lack of physical activity; nonuse of safety measures such as seatbelts and helmets; and high-risk sexual practices.

▪ *Nutrition* includes having adequate food; the meaning of food; food choices, rituals, and taboos; and how food and food substances are used during illness and for health promotion and wellness.

▪ *Pregnancy and childbearing practices* include fertility practices; methods for birth control; views toward pregnancy; and prescriptive, restrictive, and taboo practices related to pregnancy, birthing, and postpartum treatment.

▪ *Death rituals* include how the individual and the culture view death, rituals and behaviors to prepare for death, and burial practices. Bereavement behaviors are also included in this domain.

▪ *Spirituality* includes religious practices and the use of prayer, behaviors that give meaning to life, and individual sources of strength.

▪ *Health care practice* includes the focus of health care, such as acute or preventive; traditional, magico-religious, and biomedical beliefs; individual responsibility for health; self-medicating practices; and views toward mental illness, chronicity, and organ donation and transplantation. Barriers to health care and one's response to pain and the sick are included in this domain.

▪ *Health care practitioner* concepts include the status, use, and perceptions of traditional, magico-religious, and allopathic (modern, science-based) biomedical health care providers. In addition, the gender of the health care provider may have significance. (Purnell, 2002, pp. 195–196)

Purnell says, "The domains do not stand alone; each domain relates to and is affected by all other domains" (p. 195). Along the bottom of the model is "an erose (saw-toothed) line representing the concept of cultural consciousness" (p. 196). The line shows the uneven movement of an individual or organization from unconsciously incompetent to consciously incompetent, then to consciously competent, ending with unconsciously competent.

In everyday life, this means any person you meet, in a hospital, church, school, or on the street, will have a combination of domains at play in their lives and will be at different levels of cultural competence. We can't know how to reach out to them until we understand how those domains are working together in their lives. It's very similar to dealing with diagnostic co-morbidities in health care. You can't just plop a man on a gurney, send him off to back surgery and call it good. Maybe he's a former heart patient and needs special considerations for anesthesia or suffers a blood condition and needs medication to promote clotting.

In fact, being culturally agile means *adding* cultural considerations to comorbidity. Perhaps the man is already in a wheelchair or happens to be a back surgeon himself. He may believe his family must pray over him before he goes into surgery or he won't recover. (If this is not done, he and his family at the very least may be half-hearted about post-surgery care.) Maybe the man goes into surgery afraid, or refuses surgery, because he has heard stories about fewer people of his race making it out of surgery alive. All of these things affect not only the patient's health and health care experience, but an ongoing ability for caregiver and patient to work together toward successful treatment strategies.

Transforming Students Into Culturally Competent Professionals

Once the medical field came to terms with health care disparities, examined the possible reasons for them through government and industry studies, and created context through models like those described above for understanding and successfully interacting with patients, the next obvious step was to address ways to teach professional caregivers how to become more developmentally ready and culturally agile.

As I reviewed the research for my dissertation, I discovered that multiple studies have looked into developing cultural competency in students using one or more of the above models (Allen, 2010; Bednarz et al., 2010; Comer et al., 2013; Douglas et al., 2011; Giger et al., 2007; Long, 2012). Since the focus of education in health science programs has mostly been on preparation for clinical practice (interaction with patients), much of the education and training of health care providers' cultural competence has focused on gaining cultural knowledge and seeking cultural encounters with a variety of cultures the provider might encounter in the course of providing care (Long, 2012).

In other words, there was more emphasis on gaining cultural knowledge and improving resources, such as those that help practitioners to communicate better in a cultural context, than on understanding one's own culture and why we have the expectations and perceptions that we have—*before* attempting to understand others.

The IOM researchers said disparities in health outcome are partially due to provider discrimination, bias, stereotyping, and uncertainty. However, there have been few empirical studies that have identified the developmental level necessary to appreciate differences in human perceptions (Altshuler et al., 2003; Huckabee & Matkin, 2012).

Altshuler et al. (2003) believe an individual health care provider's personal level of intercultural sensitivity is a predictor of the attitude the person will have in intercultural encounters. To test this idea, they assessed pediatric resident trainees' developmental level before and after intercultural training interventions. They discovered the developmental level of participants did indeed impact the effectiveness of the training intervention. The assumption is that those in the monocultural mindset levels (as measured by the IDI) did not respond as well to intercultural training interventions, and those in the transitional mindset level of minimization or above (intercultural mindset) responded more positively. This may seem obvious, but it supports the idea that individuals must examine and adjust their own cultural sensitivity in order to more effectively interact with those who are different from them.

Huckabee and Matkin (2012), in a study of students graduating from a physician assistant program, found that most students were in a minimization (transitioning in their mindset) developmental stage, which means they likely believed cultural differences are not important or don't see them at all—they emphasized cultural commonality over cultural distinctions. In this case, to help move students past the minimization stage to greater cultural competency, recommendations included enhanced instruction, such as exploring cultural assessment methods and controversies in health care differences, combined with increased clinical experiences with diverse cultures.

In a study of the way nursing students were being prepared for cultural interaction, Long (2012) acknowledged that the development of cultural competence has been a goal of nursing accreditation and approval boards. However, the study showed there was little empirical evidence that efforts to develop cultural competence were effective. This created a gap in effectively preparing health care providers to care for patients in the 21st century.

To become culturally competent, individual health care providers need to be educated in environments that have created a *climate of respect for diversity* (Long, 2012). Such a climate is fostered when a medical or educational institution recruits faculty, staff, and students whose differences are regarded by leaders and managers as assets to be integrated, with the goal of enhancing the organization's effectiveness, rather than as issues to be confronted (Douglas et al., 2011). According to Long (2012), future health care workers are not able to develop the needed level of cultural competence unless they are taught and led through the process. Development needs to occur in colleges where diversity is embraced, and students need to be guided by faculty and staff who are developmentally able to teach and engage them in a process of growth and development (Montenery et al., 2013).

Some studies indicated that when health care faculty and staff seek ways to prepare graduates to live in and contribute to an increasingly global society, the faculty and staff become more aware of the need to enhance their own ability to effectively teach cultural competence (Comer et al., 2013; De Leon Siantz, 2008; Long, 2012). This has created a body of research showing that effective cultural competence begins with educators. To teach diverse student populations and effectively ensure their success as culturally competent professionals, health sciences colleges must embark on a comprehensive process to achieve a suitable level of transformation in their faculty and staff (Montenery et al., 2013; Sealey et al., 2006; Starr et al., 2011).

A few studies have looked specifically at faculty level of cultural competence in health care as an antecedent to student cultural competence (Sealey et al., 2006; Wilson et al., 2010). Researchers Sealey et al. (2006) suggested faculty should be urged to participate in continuing education programs on cultural competence to improve their knowledge. They stated that the continuing education programs need to be combined with cross-cultural encounters to substantially improve overall cultural competence. The study conducted by Wilson et al. (2010) indicated that cultural competence in faculty is a process and that new knowledge must be part of that process.

On the other hand, some researchers have pointed to the idea that cultural competence may have little to do with what the individual provider *knows* about culture and culturally diverse patients, and rather has more to do with the provider's personal beliefs and values. Changing the habitual beliefs and behaviors of adults is difficult when the changes require them to first confront their personal biases, stereotypes and assumptions (Comer et al., 2013, p. 90).

Campinha-Bacote's, Giger and Davidhizar's, and Purnell's models all are needed and have merit. However, none of them looks at the developmental level necessary before an individual health care provider can successfully engage with people from all walks of life. As mentioned before, I believe, Campinha-Bacote's model comes closest. Furthermore, none of the models, nor the IDI, explores what it takes for someone to *desire* to grow above minimization.

For people facing the challenges of diversity in other arenas outside of health care, the lesson is that a leader, teacher, pastor, parent, or coach must be developmentally ready to assist in increasing the cultural competence of those they lead. The task before us is to figure out how to apply all of this knowledge to the development of an inclusive mindset.

As boundaries between nations and peoples fall away due to improvements in technology and many other things, the United States is becoming more and more diverse as a nation. Other nations are becoming more diverse as well, and most of us are finding it's necessary to deal with others who are different from us. It's not that we aren't aware of this. In schools, students learn about diversity and inclusion from a very young age. So, why is it that we still have hate crimes? Why are there still people who use their power to create obstacles for those who are different from them? Why do we have such high burnout rates in people doing the work of diversity, cultural competence, and inclusion?

*   *   *

I first met Anita Rowe, PhD, and Lee Gardenswartz in 1999 when I attended the Society for Human Resource Management's Certification Course on Diversity and Inclusion. Anita and Lee were the facilitators. I felt an instant bond with them. They were warm, passionate educators who had been doing the work of diversity and inclusion since the early 1970s when Los Angeles desegregated its school systems and created the LA Unified School District. What I absolutely loved about their approach was the practical nature of their way of developing diversity and inclusion in an organization. I was so impressed with them that, when we started the diversity initiatives at Bryan Health, I invited them to present a workshop to our senior leaders and the hospital's newly created diversity council.

They helped us "prepare the ground" for the "seed of inclusion," as they called it. They became my mentors and supported my efforts at Bryan. They were the ones I called when I had questions or challenges. They listened and guided without judgement.

Fast forward to 2009. I received an email from Anita and Lee saying they had some new material they wanted to share with me. They had worked with friend and colleague, Dr. Jorge Cheborque, director of the Staff Counseling Center at UCLA, to write a book and create a train-the-trainer course called Emotional Intelligence for Managing Diversity. I was intrigued by what they shared about emotional intelligence (EQ) and wondered how it might apply to the search for cultural competence.

Dr. Brislin (2000), in his book, *Culture's Influence on Behavior*, states, "We have our strongest emotional reactions when our cultural values are violated or ignored." It made sense to me that emotional intelligence would play a role in the way we manage differences, both individually and organizationally. Knowing Dr. Brislin's and others' research, I sensed that EQ had the potential to be very powerful in developing a shift in mindset. But would it really help when it came to the practicalities of guiding others through personal change? Through my own research, I learned the answer to that question. I now know how EQ helps people shift into a more culturally competent mindset (we'll dive into that in the next chapter).

I added the principles of EQ to what I already knew about diversity, mindset shifting, cultural awareness, and so forth, and I felt the pieces were coming together nicely. But, once more, I realized a piece was missing. Human beings' emotions are completely different from our psyches—the mind and its psychology.

* * *

About halfway through the coursework for my PhD, I took a class with Dr. Fred Luthans, the world-renowned organizational behaviorist. In his class, I began learning about psychological capital (PsyCap) and all the related research. I was fascinated by the research behind PsyCap because I already was wondering how a person's psychological state impacts their willingness to do the hard work of transformation.

In Dr. Luthans' class, I also learned about the earliest theories of organizational behavior—how people in organizations behave when they come together. We studied Mary Parker Follet (mother of modern management), Fredrick Taylor (father of industrial efficiency), Abraham Maslow (famed for his hierarchy of needs), Fred Luthans and his colleagues (founders of the PsyCap theory), and many others. All of these individuals sought to better understand employee motivation, work performance, and job satisfaction.

The research is focused on how a person achieves a state of psychological presence where it operates as a strength. A clue is found in the work of positive psychologist Csikszentmihalyi, who stated (as cited in Luthans, Youssef, et al., 2007):

> Positive psychological state is a capital that is developed through a pattern of investment of psychological resources that results in obtaining experiential rewards from the present moment while also increasing the likelihood of future benefit... When you add up the components, experiences and capital, it makes up the value. (p. 542)

Thus, PsyCap is a higher-order construct. In other words, psychological capital is built through the development of these positive psychological qualities. I theorized that individuals who have higher PsyCap are more likely to intentionally work toward transforming their mindset from denial and defense, through minimization to acceptance, adaptation, and integration (the DMIS)—from a monocultural to an intercultural mindset. But what is it about PsyCap, I asked myself, that would cause that to happen?

In an article in the *Journal of Management*, Youssef and Luthans (2007) say:

> [High Psychological Capital is] an individual's positive psychological state of development that is characterized by:
>
>   1. having confidence (self-efficacy) to take on and put in the necessary effort to succeed at challenging tasks;
>   2. making a positive attribution (optimism) about succeeding now and in the future;
>   3. persevering toward goals and, when necessary, redirecting paths to goals (hope) in order to succeed; and
>   4. when beset by problems and adversity, sustaining and bouncing back and even beyond (resilience) to attain success. (p. 775, quote is reformatted for ease of reading)

In other words, to develop the positive qualities that make up higher PsyCap, we have to make a habit of "investing psychological resources" with an expectation that the result will be positive reward. The exciting part is that this is developable in human beings of all ages. However, some will never make the effort to gain such valuable qualities unless they are encouraged to do so.

To really understand how PsyCap works and be able to apply it in our daily lives, it is important to first drill down a little deeper and learn about the scientific research and background supporting each of the four states of PsyCap. These are human qualities that exist within each of us in differing amounts for a variety of reasons. The research confirms what the four qualities are, how they come about and what they can do for us as human beings. The work of Luthans, Youssef et al. (2007) brought together others' scientific research and describes the theoretical basis of each:

> *Self-efficacy* is founded on the work of Albert Bandura and his social cognitive theory. PsyCap self-efficacy is defined as the "individual's conviction...about his or her abilities to mobilize the motivation, cognitive resources, and courses of action needed to successfully execute a specific task within a given context" (Bandura, 1994, p. 38). One's state of self-efficacy is defined by how capable *we believe we are* of doing, understanding, or achieving what we want.
>
> *Hope*, based on Snyder's work, is defined as "a positive motivational state that is based on an interactively derived sense of successful (a) agency (goal-oriented energy) and (b) pathways (planning to meet goals)" (p. 66). This is our ability to see the way clear to positive outcomes (Luthans, Youssef, et al. 2007).
>
> *Optimism* is primarily founded in the work of Seligman and Csikszentmihalyi. PsyCap optimism is defined as "two crucial dimensions of one's explanatory style of good and bad events: permanence and pervasiveness" (Seligman, 2002, p. 91). As opposed to simply having hope, optimism is our capacity to explain the reasons behind things that happen in life and willingness to take positive action.
>
> *Resilience*, rooted in Coutu's work, is defined as "the capacity to rebound or bounce back from adversity, conflict, failure, or even positive events, progress, and increased responsibility" (Coutu, 2002, p. 112).

According to Dr. Luthans, there is a synergistic effect in PsyCap. Numerous research sources have proven that those who have high levels of the four qualities are happier, more satisfied, more engaged at work. Just as we take calcium and magnesium together so the magnesium can aid the absorption of calcium, we experience added benefits when we achieve high levels of self-efficacy, hope, optimism, and resilience all together. Something happens inside a person who is high in all four that makes them exponentially healthier, happier, more satisfied with life, and more productive.

As I sat in Dr. Luthans' class, I wondered: If someone tests low in the IDI but is high in PsyCap does that mean they will have a *greater desire to engage* to raise their developmental level, even if they have not figured out how to do it yet? Furthermore, does it mean they will be *more willing* to put themselves out there, admit they need to transform, and do the hard work necessary to become inclusive in their mindset?

In 2010, when I administered the IDI to the students, staff, and faculty at Bryan college, I hadn't measured their psychological state. Once I learned about and understood PsyCap, I really wanted to know how it might have impacted a shift in the mindset of participants who had raised their developmental level since then. I believed I could uncover that information with a quantitative analysis of both IDI and PsyCap results for each participant. As with the DMIS and the IDI, the science of PsyCap came with a measurement tool—a questionnaire that results in a scoring of PsyCap level.

But I was a qualitative researcher at heart and I knew numbers wouldn't be enough. I would not gain a full understanding of how participants had changed without hearing their stories (qualitative research).

Questions

1. How does the pace of your life impact your biases?
2. What are you willing to do to grow in resilience, hope, optimism, and efficacy?
3. When have you had strong emotional reactions to something someone has done or said? What does that tell you about your cultural values?
4. Which of the four factors do you need to work most on improving?

11

At the Heart of Inclusive Mindset

The world is captured by your beauty and grace.
With unity you capture the world and space.

—S. M. Hafiz

When I was a little girl, my kind Naneh, my dad's mom, who was blind, lived with us for a few years. I loved sleeping beside her warm body. Near her, I felt safe. Beside her, the world was wonderful and I could sit for a long time listening to her stories. When I was in trouble, I would try to hide under her big dress. And I would help her in whatever way I could. I loved my Naneh more than words can express.

Because of my deep love for Naneh, I wanted to know what it was like to be blind. Often, as I walked home from school, I would close my eyes and tie a handkerchief over them so I could experience blindness.

On one occasion, while I was walking blindfolded on the sidewalk a drunk man riding a motorcycle ran into me. I was thrown several feet and a large piece of the motorcycle's fender cut my leg. If I had been able to see him coming, I may have been able to jump out of the way. When I got home and told my Naneh I had been hit while trying to experience blindness, she

Becoming Inclusive, pages 141–156
Copyright © 2021 by Information Age Publishing
All rights of reproduction in any form reserved.

cried and held me close. She told me no one had ever loved her like that. I had no idea at the time, but later in life I discovered that empathy, a key attribute of high emotional intelligence, is one of my strengths as measured on the Clifton Strengthsfinder.

* * *

In 2013, I told Gina I wanted my doctoral dissertation to answer this question: "How can we ensure health care situations lead to results more like the one involving the 12-year-old Native American boy and less like the situation with my dad?" To arrive at an answer, I had to find a way to quantify why and how people change from a monocultural mindset to an intercultural mindset. I suspected the answer would help explain both positive and negative dealings with diversity, but most of all I hoped it would provide a pathway or framework—some clues—for me, my students, my clients, and many others, to help us all change our mindsets for a better, healthier, more inclusive future.

To support my dissertation, I wanted to know how a shift in mindset might have taken place for some of the IDI participants at Bryan in 2010 and 2013—and then determine whether a high level of PsyCap (a higher order construct made up of psychological states of hope, efficacy, resilience, and optimism) might have influenced the shift in IDI scores.

First, I retrieved quantitative IDI scores of all participants (faculty and staff at Bryan College) from both 2010 and 2013. I administered the PsyCap questionnaire to those who wanted to continue participation. Then I analyzed the scores to see if we could quantify a relationship between PsyCap and changes in IDI from 2010 to 2013. For the qualitative research, I selected a sampling of individuals to interview (some who had experienced a statistically significant change in their IDI scores and some who had not).

Through the interviews, I wanted to discover what had happened in each person's life (personal and professional) during that 3-year period that might have led to higher or lower IDI scores. Ideally it would have been great to see participants' PsyCap score from 2010. But I hadn't planned to use the 2010 group for research when I initially assessed them. I had conducted the 2010 assessment as part of the school's organizational plan to help faculty and staff increase the intercultural mindset of graduates. We know from research that PsyCap can be developed in individuals. While the college had not intentionally embarked on developing the PsyCap of faculty, staff, or students, I was able to learn from the interview if the participant had participated in any development related to the PsyCap constructs of hope, efficacy, resilience, and optimism.

The individuals in my dissertation study all had experienced personal and professional challenges during the 3 years between assessments. The personal challenges ranged from loss of loved ones and serious health issues (both their own and others') to children's issues and marital issues. Their professional challenges ran the gamut, from broad changes in responsibility and general uncertainty about the future to specific promotions and advancements in education. I wouldn't have known any of this had I not done the interviews. What I heard in their voices and through their tears as they talked with me doesn't show up in the numbers of a quantitative study (this is my plug for why mixed methods research is essential in complex studies).

What I heard in the interviews was not what I expected. I had been looking for explanations for changes in IDI score within each individual and their own lives. But the people who had a statistically significant change in score seemed to attribute their shift in mindset to their relationship with a specific person at the college who was high in PsyCap and already in the intercultural mindset—someone who *served as a leader* in this project. That person's name kept coming up in the interviews.

This person seemed to be the one person others would go to when they needed support during their personal and professional challenges during those 3 years. This person served as a sounding board and provided a positive outlook with hopeful words, impacting the participants in tremendously positive ways.

As you read the following details, imagine the dynamics that must have been going on in the lives and development of the people we studied—and begin thinking how these principles might apply to your own situation.

Are you a business executive, teacher, pastor, or another type of leader? Perhaps there are clues here to help you understand how you might help others grow in intercultural sensitivity and cultural competence.

Are you someone who would like to grow? Maybe this will help you find a leader who can mentor you to an intercultural mindset.

Dissertation Findings

Note: The material below has been changed from the original dissertation document for the purposes of clarity and comprehension in this book. The full dissertation, "PsyCap and the Impact on the Development of Intercultural Sensitivity of Healthcare Educators: A Mixed Methods Study," can be found at UNL Digital Commons, a free resource (Fagan, 2014).

After someone takes the IDI assessment, they must work with a qualified administrator (QA) to interpret their results and discuss an individualized development plan. The report provides language and scoring that must be explained through dialogue with the QA. Every assessment includes two measures that encompass where the person falls along the continuum of the DMIS based on their answers to the IDI questions:

Perceived Orientation (PO) "reflects where you place yourself along the intercultural development continuum. This reflects how you see yourself when you interact with culturally diverse individuals and groups" (Hammer, 2020, p. 5).

Developmental Orientation (DO) "indicates your primary orientation toward cultural differences and commonalities along the continuum as assessed by the IDI. The DO is the perspective you most likely use in those situations where cultural differences and commonalities need to be bridged" (Hammer, 2020, p. 5).

These are the three primary findings of my research:

1. Key leaders with high PsyCap and a relatively high developmental level create environments and initiatives that encourage the development and growth of others in the organization.

    One of the people in my study—we'll call this person "C"—is the participant who had the highest PsyCap score, yet C's DO did not have a statistically significant change from 2010 to 2013. C is one of the key leaders who initiated the changes during the cultural competence and diversity initiative. In fact, this is the person who fought hardest for accommodations to support nontraditional and minority students. The fight for these accommodations created the biggest challenge C experienced between 2010 and 2013.

    Several participants named C as the reason for the initiative's success. The fact that C had the highest PsyCap and a relatively high starting DO (acceptance) is potentially why others recognized them as the reason for the initiative's success. During the interviews, several participants mentioned the support they received from C. It could be surmised that high PsyCap combined with relatively high DO helped to create an environment that led to growth and forward momentum for the initiative, as well as raising the developmental levels of those in direct relationship with C.

    This person told me they were enthusiastic about engaging in multiple activities and had a strong desire to learn and grow. C's engagement in multiple learning opportunities, combined with a high PsyCap level, may be why their developmental level did not decline between 2010 and 2013. But remember, they also did not *increase* in DO. The lack of any increase in developmental level in spite of such high participation could be the result of coping mechanisms C had to employ to address pushback and resistance from others (specifically resistance and pushback from faculty about changing processes to support nontraditional and minority students).

Another factor that might explain the lack of improvement in this person's DO could have been C's immersion in a minimization culture (where most people in the group are in minimization). This finding is supported by research on social exchange theory (SET; Blau, 1964; Emerson, 1976; Erdogan & Liden, 2002). SET suggests individuals characterize themselves in terms of who they interact with and how they interact with them. C's experiences and challenges with colleagues probably could be more deeply understood through further exploration using SET.

2. Leaders with high PsyCap and relatively high developmental levels who directly supervised individuals with high PsyCap were described as having a positive impact on direct reports' developmental levels.

Another interesting way the qualitative data informed the quantitative findings in the study was the relationship between C and another participant we will call "X" who experienced the largest increase in DO (+41.57 points) and had the 4th-highest PsyCap score among those interviewed.

X cited several possible explanations for the large developmental gains they experienced from 2010 to 2013. X stated that, while there was a marked increase in work responsibilities due to the initiative, X did not feel overwhelmed, and the most support came from C (a direct supervisor), in part through the creation of an environment of trust, authenticity, and openness (the study's first finding). X said:

> I'd have to give credit to my boss—a lot of credit. When things come up, [C] is the person who comes and talks things through and [has] always been, I think, a good role model as far as "knowing the way and showing the way," which is one of our values.

The relationship between X and C is supported by other research in *authentic leadership* and PsyCap (Rego et al., 2012; Wang et al., 2014). Authentic leadership is considered a positive, genuine, transparent, ethical form of leadership (Luthans & Avolio, 2003; Walumbwa et al., 2011).

Wang et al. (2014) found that authentic leaders with high PsyCap created environments of trust, which improved the performance of followers. My present study didn't delve specifically into leaders' impact or authentic leadership, but the behaviors and attributes of C (as described by X) are consistent with previous research in authentic leadership (Reichard & Avolio, 2005).

It is also possible that X's own high starting PsyCap level was influential in propelling this person into a higher developmental level.

3. Individuals with low PsyCap experienced developmental gains if they were in close working relationships with others who had high PsyCap.

A person we will call "P" experienced the third-highest growth in DO change (+29.88) but had the lowest PsyCap score among the participants interviewed. Analysis of the interview data indicated that P was promoted into a leadership position and charged with the responsibility to create and grow a new program. P had strong doubts about being able to make that happen:

> My first instinct was [that] I felt inadequate. But one of my colleagues . . . was just very confident that I could do it . . . that I was doing it already. I was very concerned that I was going to get blindsided by what I didn't know I needed to know.

P had a great deal of support from leaders with high PsyCap who offered encouragement and support (C, R, E and several others who were not selected for the qualitative case study but had taken the PsyCap assessment as part of Phase 1 of the study). As P said:

> A lot of people accompanied me on the journey. It was different people for different things. I have many friends here, and one of them made me realize that I can be highly critical of myself. I asked them questions and they were open to me seeking their help. Collaboration is our norm.

Even though P had the lowest PsyCap, a high level of support from supervisors and other colleagues in leadership who had high PsyCap encouraged and empowered P to accept the challenges at work, and P was able to experience developmental growth. Similar findings were identified in the Wang et al. (2014) research related to performance of those with low PsyCap.

I also analyzed the qualitative and quantitative data to answer this question: *How does the qualitative case study explain the changes in organizational structures that support developmental growth in faculty and staff?*

In other words, I hypothesized that the interviews would show how changes in the college's organizational processes (involvement of the president and deans; inclusion of the initiative in the college's strategic plan) helped bring about improvement in developmental levels of those who participated in the study.

One leader in the organization was charged with operationalizing this initiative. Giberson et al. (2005) believed organizations take on the personalities of their leaders. The person selected to lead the college's initiative was described by the provost as a person who "believes it and lives it authentically."

To help college leaders gain input from both internal and external stakeholders, this leader created an internal diversity council made up of faculty and staff and an external diversity advisory board made up of community diversity and cultural competence experts. This built additional momentum to create sustainable changes in the organization's policies and practices.

During the interviews, participants mostly talked about three policy changes:

1. A new requirement for all employees to engage in ongoing cultural competence activities and educational opportunities as an essential step in ensuring faculty and staff are learning and growing in new knowledge.
2. A One Book, One College program, in which all faculty and staff, along with all students, are required to read and discuss the same book each semester as a way to create a community dialogue that challenges everyone's developmental level.
3. A variety of onsite and ongoing activities at times when the majority of faculty and staff can participate.

These are the customized changes in organizational structure that the college engaged in. The policy changes were selected based on information gained by the college leaders. Other organizations might choose different policy changes to meet the needs of their unique populations.

This information aligns with the body of research in diversity and cultural competence in health care. Richard (2000) stated that increasing diversity programming will improve organizational performance. Dreachslin (2007) observed that those leading organizational diversity and cultural competence initiatives must work to create environments in which diversity and cultural competence is fostered, encouraged, and reinforced. Wilson-Stronks and Mutha (2010) interviewed 59 hospital CEOs and discovered that diversity and cultural competence initiatives succeed when directive and support for the initiative comes from top leaders—specifically the CEO—and that the support encourages changes to current and future policies and procedures.

The body of research in intercultural competence in health care focuses on people currently providing care. Another body of research focusing on health care educators. My doctoral study was the first to look at developmental levels of health sciences faculty and staff using the IDI and PsyCap. This study was also the first mixed methods research to combine the study of PsyCap with the study of shifts in IDI developmental levels.

In my mind, one of the most significant findings of this study is that leaders with high PsyCap and relatively high DO were found to help participants increase individual developmental levels of intercultural sensitivity. It's important to realize this research focused on changes in developmental level without much emphasis on the level at which a participant began and what led up to their current developmental level.

Regardless of how the participants in my study reached higher developmental levels, it became clear to me that we need leaders who are already highly intercultural to help others change their mindset and reach for better understanding. The better we understand others who are different from us and develop an inclusive mindset, the better we can resolve difficult situations ranging from my personal, isolated experience with the nurse in my dad's hospital room to global issues such as climate change and food and water security.

We must build a global capacity for naturally and confidently embracing human differences, lest we become as endangered as many animals and plants on our planet.

*   *   *

In 2010, I scrounged up the money to attend a train-the-trainer workshop on "Emotional Intelligence for Managing Diversity" at Lake Arrowhead in California. At the end of the workshop, I knew for certain there is a connection between emotional intelligence (EQ) and creating inclusive leaders, communities, and institutions. I brought that information back and shared it with my PhD advisor, Gina, and it has influenced much of the work I've done in my career from that point forward.

At the University of Nebraska–Lincoln, I made a case for creating a new objective for the Leadership and Diversity course I'd been teaching since 2010, based on EQ: to *develop an inclusive mindset* in students, so no matter where life takes them they will have the internal capacity to manage differences well.

In the Leadership and Diversity course I frame the class around one question: "Whom would you be most afraid to bring home as your future spouse?" If you are a parent, the question would be a bit different: "Whom would you not want your child to bring home as a future spouse?"

I always ask this question during the first class of the semester and use it as a basis for the course, because I want students to grapple with the workings of leadership, diversity, and inclusion on a personal level. I want them to dig deep and become uncomfortable. I want to challenge them to move beyond theory to the practical application of the concepts they are learning with people who aren't like them.

I believe when we answer that question, we explore our unconscious bias. We are intentionally shining a light on it with the goal of moving it from unconscious to conscious bias. This allows us to notice, explore, understand, and struggle with emotions raised when we come face to face with individuals who are in "that population."

I tell my students I don't want them to *ask their parents* whom they would not want them to bring home; I want them to *think about what they've heard and seen* their parents say and do that would lead them to believe they have a bias toward certain cultures and people who are different from them. Parents want what's best for their children and often feel protective of them, and their biases come into play instinctually during times when they feel their children may be at risk. I know because I'm a mom. Asking the students to reveal their parents' biases is not a condemnation of their parents. Rather, it's a real-life exercise that helps us realize we all have biases and when we operate without admitting our biases to ourselves, we are more likely to stereotype than when we have a conscious awareness and are willing to hold ourselves accountable.

In class, students complete activities from *Emotional Intelligence for Managing Results in a Diverse World*, Anita and Lee's book with Jorge Cherbosque (Gardenswartz et al., 2010), and they discuss their activities in small groups. Through this process, the students share a type of personal information with each other that they are unlikely to share in any other class. One of the activities from the book is to write a reflection paper about the way media has impacted their perceptions of people who are different from them. I also have students watch the film *Crash* (Grasic et al., 2005) starring Sandra Bullock and many other popular Hollywood actors. I ask them to notice their gut reactions when Sandra Bullock is yelling at her husband about the Latina locksmith, or when the White police officer molests the Black woman, or when the Iranian store keeper is yelling after his store has been robbed, and use what they've been learning in class to unpack the emotions they are feeling.

It's easy to believe the stereotypes of people we have only seen in movies, news, or social media, because there is usually an element of truth in them. However, as Chimamanda Adhichi (2009) says in "The Danger of a Single Story," her TED Talk, "It's not that stereotypes aren't true; it's that they aren't the full picture." If we haven't had a real-life experience with people from a particular group, we are in danger of believing the single story we've heard and applying it to the entire group (i.e., all Mexicans are illegal, all Black men are not good fathers, all Muslims are terrorists).

Students take the IDI assessment both at the beginning and end of the semester. After they complete the first assessment, they meet with me in a private and confidential session to explore their response to the question asked of them the first day of class. Usually by the time the students meet with me, they've had a few weeks to think about it and have completed a few assignments and activities to further uncover their answer to the question. This individual meeting helps them become more comfortable with why I'm asking the question. I also share with them that, by the end of the semester, through a diversity action project, they will be asked to serve the population they've named in answer to the question.

By the end of the course, students understand that children almost always unconsciously internalize the biases of their parents. Not infrequently, some students are skeptical. They may even adamantly argue that they do not have the same biases as their parents. But through their service to the population chosen for their project, they wrestle with feelings that show them this is true. They begin to realize they must intentionally face this unconscious personal bias and work to undo it if they want to achieve any degree of cultural competence.

Katie took my class during the last semester of her undergraduate degree. She and I had wonderful discussions about her desire to live and serve abroad. When she answered the question about whom she would be afraid to bring home, she chose the homeless population. Because her kind and loving parents raised her to be a hard worker and pursue an education, she sensed that if she were to come home with someone who was homeless her parents might not approve. She acknowledged that she had internalized this same bias, and she was deeply touched and transformed by her experience serving in a homeless shelter as her diversity action project.

After graduation, Katie moved to Zambia. A few years later, she was home for Thanksgiving when her younger brother, Jake, mentioned he was a teaching assistant (TA) for my class. She had no idea he had taken the class, much less been invited to serve as a TA. I hadn't realized they were siblings. Jake told me that as he and Katie talked about their respective diversity action projects in my class, they were shocked to find out they both had chosen to serve the homeless. I believe Jake had been skeptical until that moment that parents' biases become their children's unconscious bias.

Following are the stories of three other students who have talked with me about the impact of the developmental work they've done.

Aleah is a former student and teaching assistant of mine. She became Miss Nebraska in 2015, has since married a U.S. Navy pilot, and at the time of this writing is pursuing a graduate degree in counseling. Aleah shared with me some candid thoughts about her journey toward a higher cultural mindset:

> ALEC 466 is the one class in college that changed everything for me. This material, the conversations, and the experiences in this class shifted my entire perspective. We started off by sharing our life stories with everyone. By doing so, we were able to understand why someone might value certain things based on their past experiences and how they grew up. We were able to get to know everyone in the class very quickly by knowing what shaped them into the person they are.
>
> I think everyone would like to believe they are accepting of diversity and that there is no specific population they are uncomfortable with, including myself. So, when Helen suggested that I work with people in poverty I was frustrated. I had no problem with homeless people, and I was almost offended when Helen suggested that I should research this population. After learning more about this population, I uncovered some of my own subconscious judgements.
>
> Although I had volunteered at homeless shelters before and stopped to offer my leftovers to the homeless man on the street, I realized that I have never been denied an opportunity because I didn't have enough money. I found that I had some frustration with my father for making money such a huge priority. I realized that, growing up middle- to upper-class, I was angry with homeless people "because they could be doing more to help themselves." After volunteering at People's City Mission, interacting with some of these people, I had an internal conflict.
>
> I sat down with Helen and she changed my entire perspective to help me see that although these people may look capable on the outside, their basic needs aren't being met. When a person is unsure of where their next meal is coming from, it is difficult to think about where they are going to apply for a job. I looked at the people going through the food line and kept questioning, "Why aren't you doing more to get out of here?" and Helen challenged that thought and shifted my perspective by saying, "You say why aren't you

doing more to get out of here, when some of these people are saying, 'Look how far I have come, I made it here.'"

At that point, I was overwhelmed with empathy. I questioned how I got so lucky to be born into this family. For the first time, I saw that everyone's experiences shape their values and that not everyone's common sense is common. In just one semester, I went from minimization to adaptation. My everyday interactions changed entirely. I am curious to know more about people. I want to learn what makes them who they are. I am so much more understanding and patient with others.

I am so grateful for the opportunity to take this class, as it has taught me how to get to know people for who they are not what they look like on the outside. I think back to this class almost every single day and apply it to my everyday life.

Shannon, a young lady whom I've known since she was very young, ended up being a student and later a teaching assistant after returning from a year of study abroad. She is now a mom of two, married to a pastor, and working toward her graduate degree while working full time.

I have aspired to leadership my entire life in order to gain the relevant skills to make the world a better place. In my quest to develop my efficacy and leadership capacity, I stumbled across a class taught by Dr. Fagan called "Leadership and Diversity." Although it was unexpected, my journey to becoming inclusive began right there—in an undergraduate class I needed to take to complete my minor. I learned many life-altering lessons from this class that I will always hold close to my heart. I learned about myself, about my hesitations, about my own biases. Because of one of the assignments, I took a step out of my comfort and toward the LGBTQA+ population. I learned firsthand that there was more to a person than a single, stereotypical narrative. The devout Christian who had just returned from international Bible college, volunteered in my university's LGBTQA+ resource center...and gained the gift of perspective. This was the first of several lessons I learned in Helen's class.

That class was just the beginning of several years' worth of development. After the class, I became a teaching assistant for the class that had transformed my thinking. I learned that my painful racial experiences in life shaped how I perceived and embraced my Blackness. In response, I understood that my painful experiences didn't have to evolve into life principles where I exclude, overinflate, or minimize my Blackness, and that the actions of a few don't discount the value I intrinsically have as a Black woman today. Since then, I have explored my ethnic history, embracing my Blackness and the ambiguity it requires and developing a passion to remove barriers related to equity, access, and transparency for those in my culture.

The next lesson I learned was that intercultural education is everyone's responsibility. Because I completed the assigned research project, I exposed myself to a new way of gathering information about someone's culture. To this day, I research cultures and gather information about cultures that I do not know much about from libraries, blogs, documentaries, and more. I have grown to believe the members of a specific culture are not obligated to teach everyone about their customs, rituals, and beliefs. Through this practice, I have discovered the background work we choose to do is much appreciated and is often considered a bridge when connecting with others.

I learned that while most people have good intentions, many have wavering priorities when it comes to developing intercultural competence. Development requires intentionality, reflection, and continued exposure to differences. I currently work in the honors program where I have developed workshops on emotional intelligence, leading with empathy, and teamwork that all stem from the lessons I learned when I began my journey. I even became a qualified administrator of the intercultural development inventory, the same assessment we were required to take in the class. I train businesses, individuals, and students regularly to consider these principles...and it all began in a classroom on UNL's east campus.

All of these lessons have not only supplemented my leadership, but they have also made me a better employee, friend, and person...I couldn't be more grateful.

Julie, another former student and teaching assistant, went on to earn a graduate degree and is now an extension educator for the University of Nebraska–Lincoln in Colfax County, Nebraska. Julie explained how inclusiveness has become second nature to her:

I learned so much during your leadership class as a student and teaching assistant, but the one thing that sticks out the most was how narrow my cultural view was before I took the class. I was able to expand my cultural viewpoint by volunteering as a student with the Hispanic community in Lincoln. Little did I know that I would end up working in a primarily Hispanic community, which also features community members from the Congo and Sudan. Without that class, I don't feel I would have the comfort level to interact with our communities in Colfax County. The impact that it had on my inclusive thinking was huge.

When I was a student, the class put inclusive thoughts in the forefront of my mind and made me rethink what my actions and words were. As a TA, inclusive thinking and language became more natural as I helped our students change their thought process on inclusiveness. Now, inclusiveness is second nature and I question those who don't tend to think that way. The development of my inclusiveness serves me daily in my diverse communities by allowing me to make new connections and build our 4-H and extension programs. That development serves as a strong foundation for my growth and capacity development within my profession, community, and personal endeavors. I am forever grateful for both experiences I had in being your student and TA.

∗ ∗ ∗

Since 2007, I have administered the IDI to more than 9,000 individuals from all walks of life, educational levels, and sectors of the economy, along with teaching well over 1,000 students using the IDI assessment as a pre- and post-class measure. I've learned that inclusive leaders are people who have developed attributes that enable them to connect with and use their power to help others. The synergistic effect of these attributes combined with the right environment and the desire to use their power for good gives birth to innovation, and such leaders find new ways within their own worlds to help others also become inclusive.

In 1946, Albert Einstein gave a speech on why education is the key to ceasing proliferation of nuclear weapons. Einstein believed "a new type of thinking is essential if mankind is to survive and move toward higher levels" ("Atomic Education," 1946, p. 13). In much the same way, I believe a new way of thinking and new developmental levels of cultural competence among the masses are necessary to innovatively and effectively transform people into 21st century leaders. Educators and leaders must be working toward higher developmental levels that will allow them to engage in problem-solving in a whole new way. But we have a long way to go. The developmental levels of people across the globe fall along a standard bell curve with approximately 65% of us in minimization (Hammer et al., 2003).

We need to reach toward a new level of consciousness that requires courage to dive deep into understanding ourselves (flaws and all) and then bring together people who are different from us while remaining humble and using our power for good.

As I have continued studying what it takes for individuals to be willing to embrace the challenges of developing an inclusive mindset, I've asked a few individuals to share their thoughts—people who have done the challenging work I've asked of them and have grown to become inclusive community leaders. I'd like to introduce them to you:

Jeff is chief of police in Lincoln, a medium-sized midwestern city in the United States and capital of Nebraska. I met him when he was finishing his master's degree. As part of the Developing Coaching Leaders capstone process for his degree, he worked with faculty to understand the impact of inclusion on their approach to leadership. Here's what Jeff shared regarding his growth and development:

While we discussed my upbringing, my educational background, and the lack of exposure to diversity, you provided a powerful message that resonates today: I need to be intentional about developing positive relationships with those whose life experiences differ from my own based on race, ethnicity, and culture.

As those relationships develop and trust is gained, I can see, hear, and feel the influence of these differing perspectives in my personal and professional life. Using the tools you shared helped me to gain awareness and provided the opportunity for discussion, reflection, and change. Honestly, while attending Doane and participating in the curriculum promoting inclusive leadership, I didn't see the full spectrum of how these lessons would impact my future.

In 2016, when I received an appointment to serve as Lincoln's police chief, your voice and the awareness I gained became incorporated into every facet of my life. I am constantly searching for opportunities to build positive relationships in advance of tragedy. I need to hear the voices of those we serve from the diverse representation of our community. Your instruction provided a foundation that I continue to work to build upon.

Harry, a senior pastor, contacted me to help him navigate differences between members in the multinational church where he served. The congregation held 3 different weekly services in three different languages. A large number of Chinese and Burmese members wanted to hold a special church service for those who were learning English but weren't quite up to a level of competency to fully comprehend regular services. Once a month, the three language churches held services together, and on the other weekends they held church in their own languages at different times. Three pastors worked together to make this happen. Pastor Harry's wife, Deidra, with other women in a church book club, had read the book *The Help* (Stockett, 2009) and together watched the movie based on the book. After viewing the film, they discussed how they may have been unintentionally making the Chinese and Burmese ladies feel unwelcome and making it difficult for them to integrate into the life of the church. Deidra, who knew me from my work at Bryan College, connected me to church leaders, including her husband. Over the years, we have conducted a number of different diversity activities together to help the congregation, including individual and group development work. The church created an internal group to work through some of the suggestions I gave them. Here's what Harry had to say about insights he gained during that time:

> The concept of developmental mindset around cultural differences revolutionized my ability to understand myself and not feel guilty about letting oth-

ers be who they are. As I grew in my developmental mindset to being more inclusive, I have been able to see this as a vital attribute of clergy leaders.

I seek to be a bridge builder, and the knowledge that I have gained has helped me to be more patient when there are divides created by differences. Dr. Fagan's ability to help me understand where I was in my journey and seeking to take the next steps in a diverse context is something that I had never experienced before. The internal work encouraged in me allowed me to be more open to understanding the thoughts and feelings brought on by my experiences, upbringing, and education, which then helped me to make more room in my life to accept others.

The knowledge I gained by going through this process is giving me a new and more loving vision and version of the Gospel of Jesus and the Bible. And now I am in a position to avail other clergy leaders to this type of learning.

*   *   *

That accident with the motorcycle when I was trying to experience blindness was painful, not only for me (physically) but for Naneh (emotionally), whose heart hurt to think that my desire to empathize with her had put me in danger. However, she also was deeply touched that I would attempt such a thing and it further deepened our love for each other. Now, when I think about the accident and my Naneh, it's a reminder that putting ourselves into the shoes of others can cause pain sometimes, but we must have courage, overcome the pain, and learn to understand.

Questions

1. What steps do you believe you can take to grow in your own intercultural sensitivity and cultural competence? What steps can you take to help others do the same?
2. What fears hinder you from taking a closer look at your developmental mindset? How can you overcome those fears?

12

Work in Progress

Flowers every night
Blossom in the sky;
Peace in the Infinite;
At peace am I.

—A. J. Arbery

My beloved Agha—my dad—once told me grandchildren are God's gift to parents for surviving their own children. I believe it when I think back to his delight he found in my children after enduring so many difficulties and frustrations raising me and my siblings. Now that Scott and I are grandparents, I fully understand what he was saying. It amazes me to discover from my new perspective as a grandparent how deeply my dad must have felt about Alan and Jonathan, even though he was able to spend only a short time with them in Virginia. Somehow, this small glimpse into his heart soothes my own heart.

Beckett Alan Fagan, God's wonderful gift to our family, was born October 12, 2017. We had been anticipating this momentous occasion for months. On February 17th of that year, Scott had been traveling home from

Becoming Inclusive, pages 157–166
Copyright © 2021 by Information Age Publishing
All rights of reproduction in any form reserved.

a business trip when Alan and Kacy stopped by the house to see what we were doing for dinner. They suggested we go out, so I called Scott and told him to meet us at the restaurant.

Just as I hung up, my niece, Lindsay, called to tell me she was pregnant. Lindsay is just 4 months younger than Alan, and she and her husband Steven got engaged the same day Alan and Kacy did. Their weddings were 2 months apart. The fellas made a bet: Whoever got pregnant first would have to give the other $100. As you can see, Kacy and Lindsay were ready to be Mom, but the boys were not quite ready to be Dad.

I was so excited to hear Lindsay's news that I couldn't stop talking about it. When Scott got to the restaurant, I said, "Honey, guess who's pregnant!" He looked at Alan and Kacy and said, "You guys?" I laughed and said, no it was Lindsay. We ate and talked and laughed about how Steven would be needing to give Alan $100.

When we arrived at home, Alan and Kacy said, "We have a Valentine's gift for you." Alan handed us a letter in which he had written how much he appreciated having us for parents, the lessons he'd learned from our love and hard work, and from being a child of an immigrant. He said the only way he could ever repay us was by making us grandparents. Tears were rolling down my face until the last sentence, then I began screaming and jumping up and down. The letter is framed and hangs in our bedroom, a reminder of the best news we ever could have received. As chance would have it, Lindsay and Kacy had their babies within minutes of each other.

Adding Beckett to our clan wasn't the only momentous event for our family in 2017. We also welcomed our second daughter-in-love, Liz. Jonathan married the love of his life on June 1st of that year at the Beverly Hills, California, courthouse after extenuating circumstances caused the postponement of their church wedding twice.

Liz's mom, the gracious and loving Esperanza, an immigrant from El Salvador, passed away on March 21, just 4 days before Jonathan and Liz's planned wedding. It was a terrible time of sadness and loss for all of us. I will never forget when we first met Esperanza and Liz's father, Victor. Using FaceTime and Liz as our interpreter, they lovingly told us we should not worry about our son in LA, because he had found a home in their hearts. Esperanza loved cooking for Jonathan as much as he loved eating her homemade traditional Salvadorian dishes. In a way, Jonathan's attachment to Liz, her parents and LA didn't surprise me. Months before, as I meditated and prayed for our two sons, a feeling had come over me that Jonathan would fall in love in Los Angeles and make it his home. When I met Esperanza, Victor, and Liz, we knew he was at home in their hearts and in the city.

After the funeral, Jonathan and Liz once again planned their wedding—this time for May 27th. Then, on May 21st our dear friend, Randy, who was like a brother to my husband and I and a second dad to our sons, was killed in a car accident. Jonathan and Liz came to Lincoln for the funeral instead of getting married. The pain of those months was so great, they decided they did not want to go through all the planning a third time. So, they chose to go to the Beverly Hills courthouse with Liz's Dad and extended family. We watched on FaceTime. We had a Nebraska celebration for them in September, just weeks before the birth of our grandson.

As you can imagine, throughout that year our emotions swung up and down, as life goes, and on some days, it was a challenge to stay calm and carry on.

Becoming Nana and Papa to Beckett was a whole new chapter for us. I began talking to Kacy's belly in Farsi from the moment I found out there was a little person inside, vowing I would do my best to teach the baby Farsi as I wished I had with my own boys. In his short time with us so far, Beckett has learned Nana talks to him in a different language than everyone else speaks to him. He and I have a special bond. With his hazel eyes and blonde hair, you would not think he is the grandson of an Iranian immigrant. Even though he is growing up in a small town outside Lincoln, Nebraska, he is growing up with a global mindset. Nana and Papa are working hard to help him understand the world is filled with many unique people who are different from him, and each human being matters.

In my journal on October 15, 2018, I prayed for Jonathan and Liz to have a baby. They were trying hard, and with the losses we'd had in 2017, they wanted so badly to be parents. The joy of Beckett in our lives made the baby fever even more pressing. So, I did the only thing I knew to do to help; I prayed and trusted it would happen when the time was just right.

Just a few days into 2020, Jonathan and Liz FaceTimed to say they think they are pregnant. Then, just a few weeks after everything shut down from COVID, the ultrasound confirmed our little Kash was growing and healthy. We were thrilled. We wanted desperately to jump on a plane and hug Jonathan and Liz in person, but with COVID it was not possible. FaceTime and Zoom were our saving grace. Almost every time we talked, I'd ask Liz to put the phone to her belly so I could speak Farsi to little Kash. Liz and her dad, Hugo, were speaking Spanish, Jonathan was speaking English, and I wanted to be sure he heard some Farsi too. It was a joyful time for all of us.

On October 14, just two days after Beckett's third birthday, Liz was admitted to the hospital because of high blood pressure. We were nervous and hopeful. Kash Steven Fagan joined our family, after an emergency C-section, on October 15, 2020. Liz was healthy. Kash was healthy. Jonathan was thrilled with tears rolling down his face. The joy of Kash's arrival brought us to tears and dancing. We were on FaceTime with Alan, Kacy, Beckett, Hugo, and Jonathan from the moment they took Kash to the nursery to bathe him until it was time to take him back to Mom. As the Nana of a part Salvadorian, part Iranian, and fully American child, this work continues to be personal to me.

I want Beckett and Kash to know the stories I heard from my dad and grandparents when I was growing up. I want to help them open their hearts and minds to the beauty of differences. In a way, Beckett's and Kash's births are a rebirth of me. The 15-year-old me, even the 35-year-old me, who hid my true identity, not wanting anyone to know I had been born and raised in Iran, is now openly speaking Farsi to Beckett and Kash in public. Though I do still notice the looks I get when I speak Farsi to them then turn around and speak English with no apparent accent. I giggle inside and thank God I can and do enjoy using my first language.

Maybe I'm more courageous now because I'm older. Maybe it's because I'm now a citizen and no longer afraid of what might happen to me. I'd like to think Beckett's birth has helped me feel, finally, as though I truly belong here. That joyful, beaming little face and an opportunity to share my culture with a whole new generation in a freer way helps erase the memories of pain I have gathered over 40 years, including hundreds of hateful comments saying I need to go back where I came from (one as recently as a few months ago at the time of this writing). But those experiences will always be a part of who I am, and I like who I am.

*　*　*

In the 3 decades I have been doing this work, I have learned to have patience, grace, and humility in this process of growth and development—with myself as well as with others. Until I began to truly understand how culture influences human behavior, I was just like anyone else who wants inclusive leadership attributes to come easy and quick. People often say to me (someone they perceive as a diversity expert), "Tell me everything I need to know about…" After all my research and experiences, I now understand people who say that are likely in minimization or acceptance and don't realize they need to dig deeper within themselves to find the answers. I most often respond with a question: "Who are you as a cultural being?"

The person often stares blankly or offers a response such as "I'm a mutt" or "I don't have a culture." Or they offer descriptions of places they have lived or traveled, people they've met, or languages they speak.

Although the world has made progress in many ways, we haven't widely taught the idea that all humans are cultural beings at their very core. As a result, we believe culture is related to surface qualities: people of a particular nationality, race, ethnicity, religion, age, gender or other culturally defining characteristic. As individuals, we don't always understand how culture influences our beliefs, values, and behaviors, making it that much more difficult to be open to understanding how culture has influenced others. A body of research in language-learning indicates people who are illiterate in their own language have an exponentially more difficult time learning another language. When we apply this principle to understanding culture, it becomes clear that a large majority of the population who are illiterate in their own culture likely will have an exponentially more difficult time bridging cultural differences (and developing to the level of adaptation as measured by the IDI).

The main reason I chose to pursue a PhD was to get answers to questions I believed needed to be studied to solve the problems of diversity, inclusion, and cultural competence. During my doctoral research, I conducted interviews and asked questions to better understand what happened and what led to the shift in mindset of the participants. The short answer is that people experienced great challenges, but when they had someone whom they felt supported them, the challenge led to developmental growth.

As I was conducting interviews, I was concerned if the participants would be real in sharing personal and workplace challenges with me (I had known most of them for over a decade). I was pleasantly surprised by their authenticity. Their willingness to be vulnerable is what I believe gave my study its richness and changed who I am and what I desire to accomplish. I am not the same person who began that research. The stories shared with me gave me a depth of insight about the human spirit that created an even stronger desire within me to continue to develop the potential in others. I want to be a pragmatic explorer of new ideas to help change the way we educate both present and future leaders. I want to open the door to growth and learning in my fellow human beings.

Dr. Fred Luthans once told me a practitioner and researcher needs to close the gap for people. In other words, he said, don't do consulting and teaching that aren't grounded in research. I am writing this book as a practitioner and a researcher, and I hope it helps you grow and learn, as well as help others do it, too. If you choose to apply the content of this book to the life of your organization, community, place of worship, school, or other situation or group of people, don't forget *you have to begin with you.* Until you transform your own mindset, you will have a difficult time making inclusion and cultural competence happen in your organization. No matter how much diversity you add, if you don't seek to change yourself first, inclusion most likely will elude you and others working with you. In an increasingly global economy, inclusive mindset may be the single most important quality required to lead and inspire others toward innovations to help us solve global issues such as food, water, health, education, and more.

To achieve this needed level of competence, each of us must evaluate and transform the ways we think and interact with others. To do that, we must be willing to explore how our own backgrounds, beliefs, biases, and assumptions impact our daily interactions. This depth of transformation requires courage, vulnerability, and a willingness to embark on a journey of intentional self-reflection during challenging new experiences with people who are different from us. This depth of transformation requires each of us to answer the question, "Who would we *not* want our children to bring home as their future spouse?" And then we must have the courage to hold ourselves accountable—radically accountable—to ensure that bias isn't influencing our decisions. Until we make diversity and inclusion personal, nothing will change.

I fully believe human beings are *made for connection* and becoming more inclusive is a necessity for our world. This belief about us as humans has been reinforced through my study of health care, the field where my interest and experience with diversity began. Within the health care delivery system, those who desire to heal must connect effectively with those who need healing. My purpose—as a practitioner, educator, and researcher—is to do all I can to enhance the skills of those who teach the healers and those who do the work of healing. I want to help the teacher and the healer connect more authentically with themselves. I want to help create a path to authentic connection with others from all walks of life. Ultimately, I want to help all humans find a way to genuinely connect with one another and overcome the conflicts that seem to continually trip us up.

*   *   *

What is inclusion? In the thousands of conversations I've had with individuals, whether I was teaching, completing their IDI debrief or coaching them, I've come to understand that, for most people, inclusion is interwoven with the way they feel about their environment. In this context, words with meanings related to "belonging" and "mattering" come up over and over again in the research and interviews. Lee, Jorge, and Anita address this idea in their book (Gardenswartz et al., 2010). They say leaders must meet two basic human needs, ego and affiliation, if they want to intentionally architect workplaces (environments) that result in inclusion for diverse members. In other words, the path to a more diverse workplace must include ways to help people feel that they belong and matter.

Figure 11.1 shows ranges of inclusion I have learned that people feel in their work environments. The diagram is the result of a decade of asking two questions:

1. Think of a time you worked in an inclusive environment. How would you describe it?
2. Think of a time you worked in a place that wasn't inclusive. How would you describe it?

Most often, when people answer the two questions, their stories are shared with intense emotion.

It has been an honor to listen to the stories of the individuals I have taught and consulted with. Each person to whom I administer the IDI gets to spend time with me as I coach them on the results and their path for growth and development. Many are thrilled to receive this information and wish they had known it sooner. Thousands have said this information will impact the way they interact with people in their lives, including raising

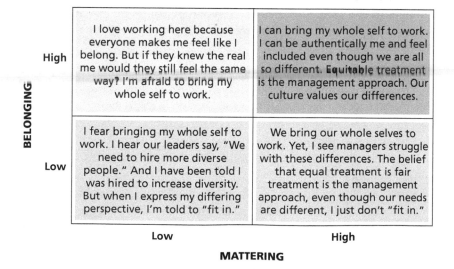

Figure 11.1   Range of inclusion. *Source:* Created by Helen Fagan (2018).

children and getting along with in-laws. As with most values we learn, inclusion begins at home. This is one of the core values I want to instill in our grandson Beckett. I'm not his mother or father, but I *am* his Nana. On the days he gets to spend with Nana, he is going to have fun and learn to value himself as a human being, as well as others who are and aren't like him. That is the greatest gift I can offer him. It's the greatest gift I can offer my students, clients, and anyone who happens to enter my life.

Doing this work is hard. Sometimes it outright sucks. But I've come to embrace the suck, because I know that through it comes growth. I encourage my students, mentees, and consulting clients to embrace the difficulties of becoming inclusive. If it doesn't challenge you, it won't change you. I have the same hope for readers of this book.

Shifting into an inclusive mindset is a lifelong endeavor. As our world changes and as we change, we encounter new things. Our brains aren't wired to automatically accept the new. In fact, most often our brains will reject what has been unknown to us unless we train our brains to enter the unknown with curiosity and without judgement while seeking to learn and understand.

As leaders, educators, health care providers, community members, and parents, we must strive to do this hard work, even though it is an Olympic-sized endeavor that does suck at times. We must lean into it and not allow ourselves to be intimidated by the difficulties associated with this challenge. We must consider ourselves Olympians in this event of life. On your personal path to cultural competence, I encourage you to be like athletes who press ahead and dedicate hours to perfecting their skill for a chance at winning the gold.

The gold you win, in this case, comes in the form of the better, richer relationships you will form because you've learned how to interact lovingly and effectively with everyone who shows up in your life. Your reward is the ability to bring healing to conversations with individuals who disagree with you. Your prize is making it possible for each of you to walk away valued, heard, and understood. I know you're thinking this sounds like an unachievable utopia. Just remember, while we may not see a pure utopia realized anywhere, striving toward it together will take us farther than we might ever have dreamed. I believe Margaret Mead was referring to this idea in her famous quote: "Never doubt that a small group of thoughtful, committed citizens can *change the world*; indeed, it's the only thing that ever has."

For the sake of Beckett and all the human beings who will come after us, I want to strive for this.

*   *   *

From a practical perspective, my research has revealed two insights I believe can be applied to help individuals.

First, leaders charged with implementing any diversity, inclusion or cultural competence initiative must be developmentally ready themselves—being at the intercultural mindset levels of acceptance and adaptation (as measured by the IDI). This is imperative if they are to bring different groups of people together to institutionalize a culture of inclusion. It is equally imperative if they are to remain steadfast in challenging the status quo. Another aspect that benefits from developmental readiness is encouraging the developmental growth of followers and colleagues. The combination of developmental readiness and high psychological capital (PsyCap) becomes a "superpower" of sorts that enables leaders to tackle difficult global issues while remaining healthy and whole. Since PsyCap is state like (meaning it is developable), as identified by Luthans and his colleagues (2007), it would be beneficial to implement PsyCap development with individuals during long-term organizational change initiatives.

In health care, Campinha-Bacote's (2002) work supports this idea, focusing on cultural desire as the first step necessary to move into cultural competence. My study added to that body of knowledge by revealing an important first step to cultural desire: developmental readiness. Training and preparing providers and health care leaders to be at the developmental levels of acceptance and adaptation, in my experience, has been the missing link in eliminating disparities in health care outcomes. One story in particular stands out to me as a perfect example. I had a lengthy conversation with a nurse manager who was in adaptation as measured by the IDI. She was working in a community hospital while pursuing a master's degree in nursing, and her goal was to become a nurse practitioner. She was required to take the IDI and do the debrief as part of her graduate classes. After the debrief, I asked her my two usual questions, along with, "What do you think helped you grow to adaptation?" She tearfully shared her story:

> We had an old local farmer who was brought to our emergency room after friends found him passed out from drinking and the heat turned off in his home. We told him he had to quit drinking and smoking, and so he was eventually transferred to the rehab part of our facility. After some time in rehab, he was released. I was in the emergency room when they brought him in again. This time, he was burned over 90% of his body. He didn't make it. I was devastated. He was such a nice guy. He was an old Czech farmer who drank. We never asked him what he wanted. We never listened to him. When he passed away, it took a toll on me. I can't help but think if we would have

asked him and listened to him instead of assuming we knew what is best, that he may still be alive today. I think we made him feel like his opinion didn't matter, and that we knew what was best for him. I had to do a whole lot of soul searching and decided that I want to do what I can to change the way people are treated. We may be experts in medicine, but the patient is an expert in their own body. We have to learn to make them feel like their opinion and wishes matter.

The second practical insight my study revealed is this: Requiring employees to engage in ongoing intercultural activities is needed to ensure faculty and staff are continuing to grow developmentally. Attaining the developmental level of adaptation is no guarantee of remaining there. Further, given the ever-changing world we live in, just because we are at the developmental level of adaptation doesn't mean we have somehow arrived, and are experts in navigating human differences successfully every time. It means our approach is to close the gap between differences by finding adaptive strategies. Adaptive strategies change as circumstances change, as we change, as culture changes. Thus, the need for ongoing developmental activities. These activities work best when they are designed to engage individuals at all developmental levels. For example, in the findings from the qualitative phase of my study, a program the college instituted called One Book, One College, has been an effective way to create a community dialogue that challenges individuals at all developmental levels. In 2018 at Bryan College, the book chosen was Jodi Picoult's (2016), *Small Great Things*. Reading this book and discussing it from a literary perspective as well as exploring the developmental shift we observe in the characters, engaged the faculty, staff, and students in seeing themselves in the characters. Fiction engages our creative brain to help us imagine the possibilities in our own lives. In my own life, I learned as much about the kind of leader I wanted to be when I read about Atticus Finch in *To Kill a Mockingbird* (Lee, 1960) as I had while listening to my dad and studying leadership research.

Questions

1. What steps do you believe you can take to grow in your own intercultural sensitivity and cultural competence? What steps can you take to help others do the same?
2. Has your answer to my original question—"Who would you not want your children to bring home and introduce as their future spouse?"—changed? Why?

Epilogue

With them the Seed of Wisdom did I sow,
And with my own hand labour'd it to grow:
And this was all the Harvest that I reap'd-
I came like Water, and like Wind I go.

—Omar Khayyam

"Mom, Nipsey's been shot. Please pray."

The call came on March 31, 2019, from our oldest son Jonathan in California as we were sitting down to dinner with our youngest son Alan and his family in their Nebraska home. My heart was torn, for I knew what a special young man Nipsey was—and how important he was to our son.

Jonathan began listening to rap music when he was about 10 years old. Knowing we wouldn't approve, he hid it from us. I found out when he was 12 and took his records from him, forbidding him to listen to the music I believed was a bad influence. Jonathan, at that young age, already was a master of argument and wizard of why.

"*Why* can't I listen?" he asked in a reasonable and mature tone I found myself respecting. "I like the beat. I don't listen to the words."

I tried to explain that his young developing brain did not need to be acculturated into the lifestyle I believed rap music represented. I finally said, "I just don't understand what it is about rap that attracts you to it."

Becoming Inclusive, pages 167–170
Copyright © 2021 by Information Age Publishing
All rights of reproduction in any form reserved.

"Mom," he said, frustrated, "things that don't make sense to you aren't always bad for me."

I shrugged and walked away with all his CDs in a box. As an educator and consultant, I had urged many people to break through their resistance and learn to be comfortable with ambiguity. But it's a whole different ball game when it's your own child throwing ambiguity at you and expecting you to take it gracefully. Jonathan's words stayed with me. The more I thought about it, the more I realized he was right. And the experience helped me grow.

As Jonathan got older, I could see a brilliant creative and entrepreneurial spirit within him. I saw his potential, but by his own admission he was a difficult child to raise. When he was 12 and Alan was 8, we created a Fagan family mission statement. Whenever the boys behaved counter to the mission statement, I would remind them about it and ask them to evaluate their choices.

Jonathan's senior year of high school was a rough one for both of us. My goal was to keep him out of trouble and keep him alive long enough to get him to college. In March of his senior year, he got in trouble at school again and lost his driving privileges. I drove him to school in tears.

"I am not enjoying this season of life with you," I said to him. "I love you, but I'm finding it hard to enjoy spending time with you." I scoured my brain for any words that might make a difference—something would pull him out of the depths and into a healthy, hopeful direction.

"What do you want to do with your life?" I asked. "You haven't even thought about college."

He was silent.

I finally said, "Jonathan, if someone called and invited you to something, what thing would be so meaningful to you that you would never miss it or be late?"

He said it would have something to do with music or basketball. So I told him, to get his car back, he needed to find a career and education related to music or basketball. A week later, he showed me a book on careers for those who love music that he'd checked out from his high school library. He had marked a couple of pages: audio engineer and producer. "That," he said, "is what I want to do."

I told him to find schools that offer those degrees and we would plan a visit. He found Full Sail University in Florida and a couple of others. He requested information from the schools, and together we agreed on Full Sail. He began classes in October of 2004. In 2012, after he had earned an audio engineering bachelor's degree and a master's degree in entertainment business and marketing, we helped him move to Los Angeles. He worked at Foot Locker as a manager while trying his hardest to break into the music industry. Eventually, he quit his paid position and interned in a couple of studios until he began working full time with Nipsey Hussle.

I'll be honest, as a mother, I was so afraid for Jonathan. He worked daily in "the hood," as Nipsey called it. But the educator and social justice leader part of me was so proud of him for pursuing his dream and aligning himself with a man who was pouring his life into bettering the community. Jonathan was Nipsey's shadow for 3 years. He worked with him in the studio, on the road, and at home. They soon became so close that they felt they were brothers born to different parents. Nipsey liked to say he had been educated in the streets while Jonathan had been educated in school. The two of them bonded as they shared out-of-the-box ideas about everything from philosophy, health and athletics to faith and of course music. And both were children of immigrants. Jonathan grew close to Nipsey's entire family.

Once, when I visited, I got to hang out with Nipsey's brother Sam. I was enamored of the similarities and differences between Jonathan, Alan, Sam, and Nipsey. While I had been driving the young Jonathan to his little league basketball games and Alan to flag football practices, Nipsey and Sam had been trying to earn money selling T-shirts on the corner of Crenshaw and Slauson (named "Nipsey Hussle Corner" after his death). While Jonathan was pursuing his bachelor's degree and Alan was in high school, Nipsey and Sam were trying to stay alive on the streets of LA. Same country, all children of one immigrant parent and one American parent, totally different experiences of life. Yet, they found they were similar enough to call one another "brother."

It makes you rethink assumptions Nebraskans tend to make about Californians and assumptions Californians make about Nebraskans! Assumptions like this, unless challenged, have a way of keeping us from bridging differences and seeking to understand one another.

Jonathan and Nipsey devoured all kinds of books together. Jonathan would sometimes Facetime me from Nipsey's place while he was waiting for Nipsey to get ready for a meeting. I usually got a chance to chat with Nipsey for a few minutes before Jonathan hung up. On occasion I'd pray with them. Nipsey called me "Moms." He told me how much he loved and admired Jonathan. And I told him Jonathan felt the same way about him.

Never in my wildest dreams did I think I would learn anything from a rapper. Yet, Nipsey taught me that in my quest to become inclusive, I still had work to do. I thought I knew what someone who grew up on the streets and created rap music was about. I thought to become an inclusive leader you had to go through schooling. In September 2018, as I sat with Jonathan in a studio and listened to people talk about Nipsey as they were filming a documentary about him, I was reminded that education happens everywhere all the time, in many different forms. I was also reminded that a college education, seen by many as an essential path to self-sufficiency in this country, sometimes can create a destructive superiority mindset toward the uneducated or those educated in a different way.

I mentioned to that group of audio engineers, producers, and artists who had collaborated with Nipsey on a Grammy-nominated album that, as they talked about Nipsey, I thought I was listening to them describe a transformational servant leader. They told me Nipsey always thought about the group and helped everyone he worked with. Several people who were interviewed for the documentary spoke of his humility, a highly valued leadership attribute. After his death, I learned about more things Nipsey did that he didn't want accolades for. As I heard the stories about his dedication to the community, to creating a better place for others in the roughest part of Los Angeles, I realized I cannot call myself inclusive just because I have a PhD or teach in this area. I must continue to do the work of inclusion inside myself. I must hold myself accountable for the biases I still have and the times when I stereotype others.

My mom's words ring true: As long as I have breath, I am a work in progress.

References

Adichie, C. N. (2009, July). *The danger of a single story*. TED Conferences.

Agency for Healthcare Research and Quality. (2016). *2015 National healthcare quality and disparities report and 5th anniversary update on the national quality strategy*. Agency for Healthcare Research and Quality. https://www.ahrq.gov/sites/default/files/wysiwyg/research/findings/nhqrdr/nhqdr15/2015nhqdr.pdf

Alexander, M. (2012). *The new Jim Crow: Mass incarceration in the age of colorblindness*. New Press.

Allen, J. (2010). Improving cross-cultural care and antiracism in nursing education: A literature review. *Nurse Education Today, 30*(4), 314–320.

Altshuler, L., Sussman, N. M., & Kachur, E. (2003). Assessing changes in intercultural sensitivity among physician trainees using the intercultural development inventory. *International Journal of Intercultural Relations, 27*(4), 387–401.

Atomic Education Urged by Einstein: Scientists in Plea for $200,000 to Promote New Type of Essential Thinking. (1946, May 25). *The New York Times*, 13.

Ayas, H. M. (2006). *Assessing intercultural sensitivity of third-year medical students at The George Washington University* (UMI No. 3237032) [Doctoral dissertation, George Washington University]. Dissertation Abstracts International.

Bandura, A. (1994). *Self-efficacy*. Academic Press.

Bass, B. M., & Avolio, B. J. (Eds.). (1994). *Improving organizational effectiveness through transformational leadership*. Sage.

Bass, B. M., & Riggio, R. E. (2005). *Transformational leadership* (2nd ed.). Erlbaum.

Batalova, J., Blizzard, B., & Bolter, J. (n.d.). *Frequently requested statistics on immigrants and immigration in the United States*. Migration Policy Institute.

Becoming Inclusive, pages 171–176
Copyright © 2021 by Information Age Publishing
All rights of reproduction in any form reserved.

https://www.migrationpolicy.org/article/frequently-requested-statistics
-immigrants-and-immigration-united-states#CurrentandHistoricalNumbers
andShares

Beck, D., & Cowan, C. (1996). *Spiral dynamics: Mastering values, leadership, and change: Exploring the new science of memetics.* Blackwell Business.

Bednarz, H., Schim, S., & Doorenhos, A. (2010). Cultural diversity in nursing education: Perils, pitfalls, and pearls. *Journal of Nursing Education, 49*(5), 253–260.

Bennett, M. J. (1986). A developmental approach to training for intercultural sensitivity. *International Journal of Intercultural Relations, 10*(2), 179–196.

Bennett, M. J. (1993). Towards ethnorelativism: A developmental model of intercultural sensitivity. In R. M. Paige (Ed.), *Education for the intercultural experience* (2nd ed.; pp. 21–71). Intercultural Press.

Bennett, M. J. (2004). Becoming interculturally competent. In J. S. Wurzel (Ed.), *Toward multiculturalism: A reader in multicultural education* (pp. 62–77). Intercultural Resource Corporation.

Bennett, M. (2017). *Development model of intercultural sensitivity.* IDR Institute. https://www.idrinstitute.org/wp-content/uploads/2019/02/DMIS-IDRI.pdf

Betancourt, J. (2003). Cross-cultural medical education: Conceptual approaches and frameworks for evaluation. *Academic Medicine, 78*(6), 560–569.

Blau, P. M. (1964). *Exchange and power in social life.* Wiley.

Brislin, R. (2000). *Understanding culture's influence on behavior.* Harcourt.

Brown, B. (2018). *Dare to lead.* Vermiion.

Campinha-Bacote, J. (2002). The process of cultural competence in the delivery of healthcare services: A model of care. *Journal of Transcultural Nursing, 13*(3), 181–184.

Cashman, K. (2017). *Leadership from the inside out: Becoming a leader for life* (3rd ed.). Berrett-Koehler.

Christopher, J. C., & Hickinbottom, S. (2008). Positive psychology, ethnocentrism, and the disguised ideology of Individualism. *Theory and Psychology, 18*(5), 563–589.

Comer, L., Whichello, R., & Neubrander, J. (2013). An innovative master of science program for development of culturally competent nursing leaders. *Journal of Cultural Diversity, 20*(2), 89–93.

Connerly, M. L., & Pederson, P. B. (2005). *Leadership in a diverse and multicultural environment.* Sage.

Coutu, D. L. (2002). How resilience works. *Harvard Business Review, 80*, 46–50, 52, 55.

Douglas, M. K., Pierce, J. U., Rosenkoetter, M., Pacquiao, D., Callister, L. C., Hattar-Pollara, M., Lauderdale, J., & Purnell, L. (2011). Standards of practice for culturally competent nursing care: 2011 update. *Journal of Transcultural Nursing, 25*(2), 317–333.

Dreachslin, J. L. (2007). The role of leadership in creating a diversity-sensitive organization. *Journal of Healthcare Management, 52*(3), 151–155.

Emerson, R. M. (1976). Social exchange theory. *Annual Review of Sociology, 2,* 335–362.

Erdogan, B., & Liden, R. C. (2002). Social exchanges in the workplace: A review of recent development and future research directions in leader-member exchange theory. In L. L. Neider & C. A. Schriesheim (Eds.), *Leadership* (pp. 65–114). Information Age.

Fadiman, A. (1998). *The spirit catches you and you fall down: A Hmong child, her American doctors, and the collision of two cultures.* Farrar, Straus and Giroux

Fagan, H. (2014). *Psycap and impact on the development of intercultural insensitivity development in healthcare educators: A mixed methods study* [Unpublished manuscript]. Department of Agricultural Leadership, Education and Communication. University of Nebraska–Lincoln.

Gardenswartz, L., Cherbosque, J., & Rowe, A. (2010). *Emotional intelligence for managing results in a diverse world: The hard truth about soft skills in the workplace.* Nicholas Brealey.

Giberson, T. R., Resick, C. J., & Dickson, M. W. (2005). Embedding leader characteristics: An examination of homogeneity of personality and values in organizations. *Journal of Applied Psychology, 90*(5), 1002–1010.

Giger, J., & Davidhizar, R. (2002). The Giger and Davidhizar transcultural assessment model. *Journal of Transcultural Nursing, 13*(3), 185–188.

Giger, J., Davidhizar, R., Purnell, L. Harden, J. T., Phillips, J., & Strickland, O. (2007). American Academy of Nursing expert panel report: Developing cultural competence to eliminate health disparities in ethnic minorities and other vulnerable populations. *Journal of Transcultural Nursing, 18*(2), 95–102.

Grasic, M., Korbelin, J., Nunan, T., Reimer, A. (Producers), & Haggis, P. (Director). (2005). *Crash* [Motion picture]. Lionsgate Films.

Hammer, M. R. (2020). *The Intercultural Development Inventory®* (IDI v5). IDI.

Hammer, M. R., Bennett, M. J., & Wiseman, R. (2003). Measuring intercultural sensitivity: The Intercultural Development Inventory. *International Journal of Intercultural Relations, 27*(4), 421–443.

Herbert, C. E., Haurin, D. R., Rosenthal, S. S., & Duda, M. (2005, March). *Homeownership gaps among low-income and minority borrowers and neighborhoods.* Abt Associates. https://www.huduser.gov/Publications/pdf/Homeownership GapsAmongLow-IncomeAndMinority.pdf

Huckabee, M., & Matkin, G. (2012). Examining intercultural sensitivity and competency of physician assistant students. *Journal of Allied Health Online, 41*(3), e55–e61.

Institute of Medicine. (2003). *Unequal treatment: Confronting racial and ethnic disparities in health care.* The National Academies Press.

Kahneman, D. (2011). *Thinking, fast and slow.* Farrar, Straus and Giroux.

Katz, R. V., Kegeles, S. S., Green, L. B., Wang, M. Q., James, S. A., Russell, S. L., & Claudio, C. (2006). The Tuskegee legacy project: Willingness of minorities to participate in biomedical research. *Journal of Health Care for the Poor and Underserved, 17*(4), 698–715. https://muse.jhu.edu/article/206217

Lee, H. (1960). *To kill a mockingbird.* Lippincott.

Leininger, M., & MacFarland, M. R. (2002). *Transcultural nursing: Concepts, theories, research & practice* (3rd ed.). McGraw-Hill.

Li, Z. (2010,). *Making sense of "care" in an intercultural context: Intercultural competence development barriers and solutions found in Canada* [Paper presentation]. Second National Transcultural Health Conference, Calgary, Alberta, Canada.

Long, T. (2012). Overview of teaching strategies for cultural competence in nursing students. *Journal of Cultural Diversity, 19*(3), 102–108.

Lundgren, C. A. (2007). *Culturally sensitive teaching: Exploring the developmental process* [Unpublished doctoral dissertation]. University of Minnesota, St. Paul.

Luthans, F., & Avolio, B. J., (2003). Authentic leadership development. In K. S. Cameron, J. E. Dutton, & R. E. Quinn (Eds.), *Positive organizational scholarship* (pp. 241–258). Berrett-Koehler.

Luthans, F., Avolio, B. J., Avey, J. B., & Norman, S. M. (2007). Positive psychological capital: Measurement and relationship with performance and satisfaction. *Personnel Psychology, 60*(3), 541–572.

Luthans, F., Youssef, C. M., & Avolio, B. J. (2007). *Psychological capital.* Oxford University Press.

Manyika J., Bughin, J., Lund, S., Nottebohm, O., Poulter, D., Jauch, S., & Ramaswamy, S. (2014, April 1). *Global flows in a digital age.* McKinsey & Company. https://www.mckinsey.com/business-functions/strategy-and-corporate-finance/our-insights/global-flows-in-a-digital-age#0

Meet the Press News Show. (1960, April 17). Available at: https://www.youtube.com/watch?v=1q881g1L_d8

Montenery, S. M., Jones, A. D., Perry, N., Ross, D., & Zoucha, R. (2013). Cultural competence in nursing faculty: A journey, not a destination. *Journal of Professional Nursing, 29*(6), e51–e57. https://doi.org/10.1016/j.profnurs.2013.09.003

Moodian, M. (2009). *Contemporary leadership and intercultural competence: Exploring the cross cultural dynamics within organizations.* Sage.

Northhouse, P.G. (2013). *Leadership: Theory and practice* (6th ed.). Sage.

Office of Minority Health. (n.d.). *What is cultural competency?* http://minorityhealth.hhs.gov/templates/browse.aspx?lvl=2&lvlid=11

Papadopoulos, R. (2003). The Papadopoulos, Tilki, and Taylor model for the development of cultural competence in nursing. *Journal of Health, Social and Environmental Issues, 4,* 5–7.

Picoult, J. (2016). *Small great things.* Ballantine Books.

Purnell, L. (2002). The Purnell model for cultural competence. *Journal of Transcultural Nursing, 13*(3), 193–196.

Quinn, R. E. (1996). *Deep change: Discovering the leader within.* Jossey-Bass.

Rego, A., Sousa, F., Marques, C., & Pina e Cunha, M. (2012). Authentic leadership: Promoting employees' psychological capital and creativity. *Journal of Business Research, 65*(3), 429–437.

Reichard, J., & Avolio, B. J. (2005). Where are we? The status of leadership intervention research: A meta-analytic summary. In W. L. Gardner, B. J. Avolio, & F. O. Walumbwa (Eds.), *Authentic leadership theory and practice: Origins, effects and development* (pp. 203–226). Elsevier Press.

Richard, O. C. (2000). Racial diversity, business strategy, and firm performance: A resource-based view. *The Academy of Management Journal, 43*(2), 164–177.

Samovar, L. A., & Porter, R. E. (Eds.). (1997). *Intercultural communication: A reader* (eighth ed.). Wadsworth.

Sealey, L., Burnett, M., & Johnson, G. (2006). Cultural competence of baccalaureate nursing faculty: Are we up to the task? *Journal of Cultural Diversity, 13*(3), 131–140.

Seligman, M. (2002). *Authentic happiness: Using the new positive psychology to realize your potential for lasting fulfillment.* Simon & Schuster.

Skloot, R. (2010). *The immortal life of Henrietta Lacks.* Crown.

Starr, S., Shattell, M., & Gonzales, C. (2011). Do nurse educators feel competent to teach cultural competency concepts? *Teaching and Learning in Nursing, 6*(2), 84–88.

Stevenson, B. (2014). *Just mercy: A story of justice and redemption.* Spiegel & Grau.

Stockett, K. (2009). *The help.* Penguin House.

Tweedy, D. (2016). *Black man in a white coat: A doctor's reflections on race and medicine.* Picador.

U.S. Department of Health and Human Services. (1985). Report of the Secretary's Task Force on Black & Minority Health. https://www.minority health.hhs.gov/assets/pdf/checked/1/ANDERSON.pdf

U.S. Public Health Service Syphilis at Tuskegee. (2015, December 22). *The Tuskegee timeline.* https://www.cdc.gov/tuskegee/timeline.htm

Walumbwa, F. O., Luthans, F., Avey, J., & Oke, A. (2011). Authentically leading groups: The mediating role of collective psychological capital and trust. *Journal of Organizational Behavior, 32*(1), 4–24.

Wang, H., Sui, Y., Luthans, F., Wang, D., & Wu, Y. (2014). Impact of authentic leadership on performance: Role of followers' positive psychological capital and relational processes. *Journal of Organizational Behavior, 35*(1), 5–21.

Wikipedia. (n.d.). Henrietta Lacks. In *Wikipedia.* Retrieved July 25, 2018 from https://en.wikipedia.org/wiki/Henrietta_Lacks

Wilson, A., Sanner, S., & McAllister, L. (2010). A longitudinal study of cultural competence among health science faculty. *Journal of Cultural Diversity, 17*(2), 68–72.

Wilson-Stronks, A., & Mutha, S. (2010). From the perspective of CEOs: What motivates hospitals to embrace cultural competence? *Journal of Healthcare Management, 55*(5), 339–351.

Witherell, S. (2015, November 16). *Open doors 2015 report.* The Power of International Education. https://www.iie.org/Why-IIE/Announcements/2015/11/2015-11-16-Open-Doors-Data

World Health Organization. (2013, November 11). *Global health workforce shortage to reach 12.9 million in coming decades.* http://www.who.int/mediacentre/news/releases/2013/health-workforce-shortage/en/

Youssef, C. M., & Luthans, F. (2007). Positive organizational behavior in the workplace: The impact of hope, optimism, and resiliency. *Journal of Management, 33*(5), 774–800.

About the Author

Helen **Abdali Soosan Fagan** is a leadership, diversity, and inclusion scholar and practitioner. She is the founder of Global Leadership Group, which provides consulting and leadership coaching to organizations, communities, and executives interested in becoming an inclusive leader or launching a Diversity and Inclusion initiative.

She combines her scholarship and practice with her personal experience as an immigrant from Iran. Dr. Fagan came to the United States, as an international student, at age 15, just months before the Iran Hostage Crises.

In addition to a PhD in Human Sciences with specialization in Leadership from University of Nebraska-Lincoln, Dr. Fagan holds multiple certifications in diversity, emotional intelligence, and is a trained executive coach. Dr. Fagan studied international economics and British political economy at Oxford University during the formation of the EU. Before academia, she created and led diversity and cultural competence initiatives in a large health care system. She has served as a coach, mentor, and sounding board for leaders from all walks of life.

Dr. Fagan's expertise in developing inclusive leaders, organizations, and communities has enabled her to speak in multiple nations and at last count four continents. Dr. Fagan's passion is to develop inclusive leaders who create better tomorrows. She and her husband reside in Lincoln, Nebraska. They are the proud parents of two married sons, and two grandsons.

Becoming Inclusive, page 177
Copyright © 2021 by Information Age Publishing
All rights of reproduction in any form reserved.

CPSIA information can be obtained
at www.ICGtesting.com
Printed in the USA
LVHW052146130222
710950LV00002B/3

9 781648 025235